Da Capo Press Series in
## GRAPHIC ART
General Editor: A. Hyatt Mayor
*Curator Emeritus of Prints, Metropolitan Museum of Art*

# Volume 10

# PRINTS
## AND VISUAL
## COMMUNICATION

# PRINTS
## AND VISUAL
## COMMUNICATION

### By William M. Ivins, Jr.
*Late Curator of Prints*
*Metropolitan Museum of Art*

**THE M.I.T. PRESS**
Cambridge, Massachusetts, and London, England

This M.I.T. paperback edition of *Prints and Visual Communication* is an unabridged republication of the first edition published in 1953 by Harvard University Press. It is reprinted by special arrangement with Routledge & Kegan Paul, Ltd.

The publishers are grateful to the Prints Division, New York Public Library, and to the Department of Prints, Metropolitan Museum of Art, for providing new photographs for a number of illustrations.

First MIT Press paperback edition, August 1969
Second printing, February 1973
Third printing, January 1978
Fourth printing, July 1980

ISBN 0 262 59002 6

Library of Congress Catalog Card Number 68-31583

TO

THE MEMORY

OF

F.W.I.

# PREFACE

THE thesis of this book grew out of a long endeavour to find a pattern of significance in the story of prints. To discover the pattern it was necessary to approach that story from a point of view which lay outside it, and to take account of values and effects that have customarily been overlooked.

For many years the writer had desired to prepare an ordered argument of his thesis, but time free for the purpose did not come until after retirement from official duties and the fulfilment of some old obligations. Slightly later an invitation to deliver a course of eight lectures at the Lowell Institute of Boston, in January, 1950, not only gave him the inestimable benefit of a 'dead line', but caused him to shorten and simplify his argument.

The book has been written from memory, without notes. When it was finished the writer verified his quotations, checked names, dates, and a few incidents in the common reference books, and made most of the photographs for the illustrations.

The writing was almost finished when there came to hand for the first time André Malraux's *La Psychologie de l'Art*, in which part of the problem here dealt with is considered from a very different point of view and to quite another end.

The writer thanks the following friends for their many kindnesses and their patience with him: Mr. and Mrs. George Boas, W. G. Constable, Alfred E. Cohn, Dudley T. Easbey, Mr. and Mrs. N. Gabo, Walter Hauser, A. M. Hind, A. Hyatt Mayor,

# PREFACE

Beaumont Newhall, Miss Alice Newlin, Edward Milla, Mr. and Mrs. Theodore Sizer, and Thomas J. Wilson. Especially he thanks the Metropolitan Museum of Art and its staff, past and present, for innumerable courtesies. From his daughter Barbara he has received the keenest of criticism and the most affectionate and unremitting of encouragement.

The notation '(MM)' in the captions for the illustrations indicates that they have been reproduced by permission of the Metropolitan Museum of Art from originals in its collections.

Thanks to the generosity of the publishers, most of the plates have been produced by the collotype process on paper other than that used for either the line blocks or the half tones. To secure the great gain in accuracy of reproduction of the fine textures of the originals thus made possible, it has been mechanically necessary to sacrifice what otherwise would have been the order of the plates in the book.

*Woodbury*
  *Connecticut*

# CONTENTS

# ILLUSTRATIONS

manner'. It was succeeded in Italy by the 'broad manner' of the painter engravers, which reached its apogee in the original work of Mantegna.

6. Portion of Mantegna's engraved Bacchanal with Silenus (MM)
   *after page* 24
   Reduced. To be compared with Dürer's pen and ink copy reproduced on the opposite page.

7. Portion of Dürer's pen and ink copy of Mantegna's Bacchanal with Silenus (in the Vienna collection)    *after page* 24
   Reduced. Mantegna engraved much as he drew with his pen. Dürer in copying him substituted his own anecdotal German calligraphy for Mantegna's simplified powerful statement of essentials. In this kind of distortion Dürer has been followed by most of the succeeding engravers, who have given more attention to the weaving of linear textures than to reporting the basic qualities of their originals.

8. Portion of an anonymous early Italian engraved copy of a drawing by Mantegna (MM)    *facing page* 25
   Enlarged. One of the first sizeable groups of reproductive engravings was made during Mantegna's life after drawings by him. In many of them Mantegna's style of drawing was closely copied, presumably because it was also the natural style of the engravers. The dots in the outlines of the impression here reproduced were made when it was pricked to take off its design on another piece of paper.

9. Portion of a primitive woodcut of St. Christopher    *page* 25
   About actual size. Prints of this type are attributed to the early years of the fifteenth century. (Reproduced from Max Lehrs, *Holzschnitte d. ersten Hälfte d. XV Jahrhunderts im K. Kupferstichkabinett zu Berlin*, issued by the Graphische Gesellschaft of Berlin in 1908.)

10. The earliest picture of a printing press. Woodcut from a *Dance of Death* printed at Lyons in 1499    *page* 26
    Reduced. (Reproduced from the facsimile of the unique copy in Claudin's *Histoire de l'Imprimerie en France*, Paris, Imprimerie Nationale, 1900 ff.)

11. Woodcut from Torquemada's *Meditationes*, Rome, 1473 (MM)
    *page* 30
    Reduced. This woodcut also appeared in the edition of 1467—the first book printed from type in Italy which contained printed illustrations. They were printed with the type. It was also the first book printed anywhere which contained illustrations that purported to represent specifically located particular things—in this instance some wall decorations in the Church of Santa Maria sopra Minerva which no longer exist.

ILLUSTRATIONS

12. Portion of a woodcut from Valturius's *De re militari*, Verona, 1472 (MM) *page* 31

Reduced. This was the first book illustrated with printed pictures of machinery—this one representing a primitive and doubtless imaginary 'Gatling gun' with eight barrels. The roughly inked blocks were carelessly impressed by hand in blanks left for the purpose in the printed text.

13. Woodcut of 'Asparagus agrestis', from the herbal of the *Pseudo-Apuleius*, Rome, n.d. (*c.* 1483) (MM) *page* 32

About actual size. This was the first illustrated printed herbal. Its woodcuts were rough copies of the drawings in a ninth-century manuscript.

14. Portion of a head of Christ by the early German Master E. S. (MM) *facing page* 32

Enlarged. Showing a step in the early German development from the goldsmith's type of engraving towards a systematized calligraphic linear system.

15. Torso from Mantegna's engraving of the Risen Christ between SS. Andrew and Longinus (MM) *after page* 32

Enlarged. The final development of Mantegna's linear system in engraving. Mantegna's prints had a great influence on design, but counted for little in the subsequent development of the linear structures of professional reproductive engraving. His manner of drawing and shading required powerful draughtsmanship and provided little opportunity for the display of the mere craftsman's skill in routine manipulation.

16. Torso from Dürer's engraving of Adam and Eve (MM) *after page* 32

Enlarged. Dürer's masterpiece of engraved representation of the naked human body. It shows the development of his calligraphic drawing under pressure of his love of detail and his pride in the manual adroitness with which he could lay lines of the greatest fineness with the sharp point of his engraving tool. In spite of his genius, he was probably the greatest of the writing masters—and it is to this that he owes much of his popular fame.

17. Torso from Dürer's woodcut of The Trinity (MM) *after page* 32

Enlarged. Dürer's masterpiece of woodcut representation of the naked human body. Its linear system is to be compared with that of his engraved Adam and Eve. This is a remarkable rendering of a calligraphic pen drawing on the block that had been simplified to meet the exigencies of the woodcutter.

xiii

18. Figure from Marc Antonio's early engraving of Pyramus and Thisbe (MM) *after page* 32

Enlarged. An example of the coarse, rough, careless, linear system used by Marc Antonio before he had become thoroughly familiar with Dürer's work. He did not love and caress his lines as Dürer did, and neither was he a dandy as Dürer was.

19. Portion of Marc Antonio's late engraving of Jupiter and Cupid, after Raphael (MM) *after page* 32

Enlarged. An example of the linear system that Marc Antonio finally developed out of Dürer's engravings and woodcuts for the reproduction of ancient sculpture and of Raphael's designs.

20. Portion of Lucas of Leyden's late engraving of Lot and his Daughters (MM) *after page* 32

Enlarged. An example of the linear system finally evolved by Lucas, when he had emerged from Dürer's influence and fallen under that of Marc Antonio. In this he pointed the way to such later men as Goltzius.

21. Portion of an engraving of the statue of Laocoon published by Lafreri at Rome in the middle of the sixteenth century (MM) *facing page* 33

Enlarged. An example of what happened when Marc Antonio's late style fell into the hands of the unintelligent hack engravers of the print publishers.

22. Woodcut of 'Gladiolus', from the herbal known as the *Gart der Gesundheit*, Mainz, 1485 (MM) *page* 35

Reduced. This was the first printed herbal illustrated with printed pictures after drawings specially made for the purpose from actual plants. Its printer was Peter Schoeffer, the surviving partner of Gutenberg.

23. Detail from a woodcut view of Venice, from Breydenbach's *Peregrinationes*, Mainz, 1486 (MM) *page* 37

Enlarged. This was the first printed book of travel that was illustrated with printed pictures after drawings made for the purpose by one of the travellers. His name was Erhard Rewich ('Erhardum silicet Rewich'), and he was the first illustrator of a printed book whose name is known to us. This view of Venice was a folding plate, about six feet long.

24. Woodcut of a living-room, from Pelerin's *De Perspectiva*, Toul, 1504 (courtesy of the Pierpont Morgan Library) *page* 41

Reduced. This was the first printed book to contain the basic rules of modern perspective, and its illustrations are the earliest prints to be drawn in accordance with those rules.

32. Figure from Mantegna's engraving of the Bacchanal with the
Wine Press (MM)                                    *after page* 48

Enlarged. From an early impression showing the warmth and softness
of line caused by leaving the burr on the plate and not removing it
before printing.

33. The same figure from Mantegna's engraving of the Bacchanal
with the Wine Press (MM)                           *after page* 48

Enlarged. From a late impression printed after the burr had vanished
and the lines themselves had worn. Most of the impressions of Mantegna's plates are of this hard cold kind and give an utterly false idea
of his essential qualities. This pair of contrasting impressions has been
selected for reproduction because of the largeness of their lines.

34. The head from Van Dyck's original etching of Frans Snyders
(MM)                                               *after page* 48

Enlarged. Its linear structure is to be compared with that of Paul du
Pont's engraved portrait of Van Baelen after a sketch by Van Dyck,
on the opposite page. The originals of the two heads are closely of the
same size. This one, in its easy assured use of the inherited Rubens
formulae, has character and sharp, if summary, notation.

35. The head from du Pont's engraved portrait of Van Baelen,
after a sketch by Van Dyck. From the *Iconography* of 1645
(pr. coll.)                                        *after page* 48

Enlarged. A typical example of the standardized linear structure
evolved by the Rubens school of engravers. Here the qualities of the
Van Dyck on the opposite page have been sacrificed to a mere craftsman's delight in the pedantic slickness of a formalized and insensitive
linear net.

36. Portion of Vorstermans's engraving of 'M. Brutus Imp.', after
a drawing by Rubens 'from an ancient marble', 1638 (MM)
*facing page* 49

Reduced. Showing what Rubens in the seventeenth century thought
the proper way to reproduce a piece of classical sculpture.

37. Mellan's engraving of Samson and Delilah (MM)
*facing page* 64

Reduced. Showing Mellan's development of parallel shading as a device
for the exhibition of popularly (and easily) appreciable craftsmanship.

38. Portion of Baudet's engraving of the 'Spinello' (MM)
*after page* 64

About actual size. Mellan had engraved some statues in this manner
—which, however, reached its final development of vapidity at the

xvi

hands of such later men as Baudet in the 1680's. As a stunt, it probably bears much the same relation to draughtsmanship that Paganini's playing on one string did to music.

39. The head of Nanteuil's engraved portrait of Pomponne de Bellelievre (MM) *after page* 64

Enlarged. This ultimate example of empty and obvious linear virtuosity is generally regarded as the great masterpiece of French classical portrait engraving. As one looks at it one can almost hear the engraver saying to himself: 'Now I'll show 'em'.

40. Portion of Watteau's painting of Le Mezetin (photo. MM)
*after page* 64

Reduced. To be compared with Audran's engraving on the facing page. This half tone is not regarded as a work of art as that engraving is, but it tells much more about the original. It is to be noted how the engraving turned Watteau's portrait of a hard-bitten member of the Comédie Italienne into that of a love-lorn youth.

41. Portion of Audran's mixed engraving and etching after Watteau's painting of Le Mezetin (MM) *after page* 64

About actual size. From Jullienne's *L'Œuvre d'Antoine Watteau . . . Fixé à cent exemplaires des Premières Epreuves* (Paris, in the 1730's) —the first attempt to reproduce the oeuvre of an important painter. It was an inestimable boon to the forgers and copyists of Watteau. Blond, sparkling prints, such as this, had a great influence in succeeding French eighteenth-century practice.

42. The face from the engraving by Gaillard after the painting of 'L'Homme a l'œuillet' (MM) *after page* 64

Enlarged. The fine lines lie below the threshold of normal human vision. It is doubtful whether such work could or would have been done had it not been for the then recent discovery of photography. Gaillard was one of the leaders in the French mid-nineteenth-century revolt against the old standardized linear systems in reproductive engraving.

43. A chalk sketch by Watteau as reproduced in Jullienne's *Figures de differens characteres . . .*, Paris, in the 1730's (MM)
*after page* 64

About actual size. This skilful but simple rendering in mixed etching and engraving was made by the Count Caylus, a gifted amateur, who made many reproductions of drawings and other works of art of all times and schools. He only reproduced things that amused him. Wealthy, witty, debauched,—soldier, man of letters, archaeologist, critic, and cruel art patron,—Caylus's influence is still visible in conservative contemporary taste.

44. The central figures from Rembrandt's mixed etching and dry point of the Agony in the Garden (MM) *facing page* 65

Enlarged. Showing Rembrandt's unwillingness to subordinate expression and lively draughtsmanship to a formal linear structure which would have given him both larger editions and greater popularity. It was not tidy and had no trace of the highly polished machine finish that was rapidly becoming essential to commercially successful print making.

45. Portion of a trial proof of Lucas's mezzotint after Constable's sketch of Stoke-by-Neyland (MM) *facing page* 80

Enlarged. Sharp lines, abrupt transitions, and variations of texture, i.e. brilliance and transparency, were impossible to achieve in the treacly medium of mezzotint. It only reached great popularity in England, where it became the typical technique for the reproduction of low keyed oil paintings by British artists of the late eighteenth and early nineteenth centuries. No original artist has ever adopted mezzotint as his medium of expression.

46. Portion of Goya's pure aquatint 'Por que fue sensible' (pr. coll.) *after page* 80

Enlarged. Although aquatint, usually in combination with etching, was very popular in the late eighteenth and early nineteenth centuries for the reproduction of water colour drawings, Goya was the only major artist ever to use it habitually for original work.

47. The Ecchoing Green from Blake's *Songs of Innocence*. Reproduced from an uncoloured impression of the original relief etching in Gilchrist's *Life of William Blake*, London, 1863.

*after page* 80

About actual size. Blake's *Songs of Innocence* were printed in 1789 from copper plates etched in relief. The technique came to its full usefulness when the younger Gillot combined it with a way of photographically transferring a drawing to a plate.

48. Portion of a relief print by Daumier, entitled 'Empoignez les tous . . .'; from *Le Magasin Charivarique*, Paris, 1834 (pr. coll.)

*after page* 80

About actual size. Probably made by a variety of the 'chalk plate' process. It shows how much the merit of a print depends on the man who makes it, rather than upon any particular quality of the process used. This has not been understood in the English speaking countries.

49. A tail-piece from Bewick's *Land Birds*, originally published at Newcastle in 1797 *after page* 80

Enlarged. An early white line wood-engraving. Three impressions from the same block: (1) a specially inked and printed proof on

China paper (MM) ; (2) a carelessly inked and printed impression on rough paper from the textless edition of 1800 (pr. coll.) ; (3) an impression on better paper from the edition of 1832 (pr. coll.). These three impressions illustrate the difficulties the printers had in printing Bewick's fine textured white line blocks with the papers and inking methods then available.

50. Detail of Charlton Nesbit's wood-engraving of Rinaldo and Armida, from Savage's *Hints on Decorative Printing*, London, 1822 (pr. coll.) *after page* 80

Enlarged. This impression was carefully printed on China paper mounted on the regular paper of the book. The engraver instead of frankly working in white lines as Bewick and Blake did, attempted to make his prints look like black line engravings on copper—then still regarded as the best way of reproducing pictures. But he went copper engraving one better by engraving schematic white lines across his schematic black lines.

51. Detail from the defaced block of Nesbit's Rinaldo and Armida (pr. coll.) *after page* 80

Enlarged. This impression was printed with ordinary care on the paper used for the text pages of the book. Impressions from the defaced blocks were inserted at the end of Savage's book to show that there could be no subsequent edition—but, after the blocks had been defaced and printed from in that condition, this one, at least, was promptly repaired and some impressions from it were printed with great care on China paper. In making up the copies of the book some of these later impressions got mixed with the earlier China paper ones and were used in their places in the book. Thus this very bad impression from the defaced block is actually earlier than that on China paper reproduced on the facing page from the same copy of the book.

52. Two black line wood-engravings from *Puckle's Club*, London, 1817 (pr. coll.) *after page* 80

About actual size. While the illustrations were printed on India paper mounted on the text pages, the tail-pieces were printed with the type on the paper of the text pages. The difference in quality of impression caused by the different papers is obvious. Paper adequately smooth to yield good impressions from such fine textured blocks was not available for commercial use until the end of the nineteenth century.

53. Two wood-engravings, one by Blake and one anonymous, from Thornton's *Eclogues of Vergil*, London, 1822 (pr. coll.) *after page* 80

About actual size. This was one of the earliest school text books to be illustrated with a large number of wood-engravings. Those by Blake are among the earliest perfectly free drawings done with the engraving tool on the wood. Thornton found it necessary to apologize for them in a footnote, but saw no necessity to comment on the other blocks, which are typified by the second reproduction. The blocks were printed with the type on the cheap paper of the book.

54. Portion of Harvey's wood-engraving of B. R. Haydon's painting of the 'Death of Lucius Quintus Dentatus' (MM)

*after page* 80

Enlarged. The earlier wood-engravings were so small that the difficulties in printing came from the paper and the methods of inking. This engraved block, however, was $11\frac{1}{2}$ by 15 inches in size, and was so full of blacks that until about 1821 no press was found powerful enough to print it. When finally printed, it had to be done in a very limited edition on India paper, which alone was smooth enough. By that time the block had split. A prime example of the dominance of the copper-engraved linear structure inherited from the sixteenth century.

55. The famous classical statue of Niobe and her Daughter, from the *Penny Magazine* in 1833                                         *after page* 80

Reduced. The *Penny Magazine*, started in 1832 by Charles Knight, was the first cheap illustrated English weekly, and rapidly reached a circulation of 200,000 copies. This engraving on wood was coarsely worked to be printed rapidly on cheap paper in a power press. Far from being a deliberate caricature, it was a serious attempt to bring information and culture to the greater British public.

56. Portion of a wood-engraving of a drawing on the block by Daumier (pr. coll.)                                         *facing page* 81

Enlarged. While in England they were making pale wood-engravings like those in the Tennyson of 1857, the French began to make more full-bodied illustrations. This one appeared in *Le Monde Illustré* in the middle 1860's. It was engraved by Maurand. At the beginning of the present century such prints as this had great influence on French original wood-engraving, e.g. in the work of Lepere, who once owned the rubbed proof from which this reproduction is taken.

57. Portion of the wood-engraving after Giotto's 'The Salutation', from *Arena Chapel Padua*, London, 1860 (MM)

*facing page* 96

About actual size. The set of wood-engravings from which this is taken introduced Giotto's paintings in the Arena Chapel to the English speaking world. The accompanying text was written by Ruskin. A perfect example of how the mid-Victorian engravers unconsciously transformed figures from the distant past into masqueraders from Barchester Towers. From the time when Dürer translated Mantegna into Nuremberg German to this translation of Giotto into 'refined' nineteenth-century English transformation of this kind was inevitable in all printed copies or reproductions of works of art.

Linton. The apogee of English reproductive white line engraving on wood was reached in the last quarter of the nineteenth century in such prints as this—freely drawn with the engraving tool through a photographic image on the block. The advent of the cross line half-tone screen for photo-mechanical reproduction, in the 1890's, put an end to this kind of work.

thought adequate to represent the things that Winckelmann wrote about. They explain a great deal of old aesthetic theorizing and values. Today such a print as this smacks, not of any ancient classical work, but of the decorations which similar reproductions inspired in nineteenth-century German beer halls. Its 'original', about which Winckelmann's was comically enthusiastic, was actually an eighteenth-century fake.

# ILLUSTRATIONS

still dominated by the formal linear scheme invented by the engravers on copper at the end of the sixteenth century. 'A certain conservatism' may be said to be the distinguishing mark of all text-book illustration even to the present day.

82. A head from the 'etched state' of the print after Moreau le jeune for 'Les Délices de la Maternité' in the set of engravings known as the *Monument du Costume*, Paris, 1777 (MM)

*facing page* 133

Enlarged. Preliminary etching of this kind was known as 'forwarding'. It played little or no part in the effect of the finished print. The taste of the time did not approve such summary and expressive use of line in its printed pictures.

83. The same head from 'Les Délices de la Maternité', after it had been finished by the engraver and by him reduced to the accustomed linear system. That this killed all its colour and expression was not thought a matter of importance (MM)

*facing page* 140

84. A modern half-tone, made for this book, of a detail from Rembrandt's painting of 'An Old Woman Cutting her Nails' (photo. MM) *facing page* 141

Modern panchromatic photographic emulsions and modern cross line half-tone process, together with the improvements in presses and press work and in the making of very smooth papers, have made possible the illustration of cheap books and magazines with reproductions such as this, in which *the actual surfaces of the objects reproduced are made visible*. The lines and dots of the process are too small to be seen by the unaided human eye, and no longer remain to distort and falsify the pictorial reports as they did in all the earlier hand-made graphic processes and in the early half-tones. In this half-tone there are 133 dots to the linear inch.

# I

## INTRODUCTION

## THE BLOCKED ROAD TO

## PICTORIAL COMMUNICATION

I N 1916 and 1917, when the department of prints of the Metropolitan Museum of Art in New York was being started, there was much talk and argument about what the character of its collection should be. In the course of those discussions I became aware that the backward countries of the world are and have been those that have not learned to take full advantage of the possibilities of pictorial statement and communication, and that many of the most characteristic ideas and abilities of our western civilization have been intimately related to our skills exactly to repeat pictorial statements and communications.

My experience during the following years led me to the belief that the principal function of the printed picture in western Europe and America has been obscured by the persistent habit of regarding prints as of interest and value only in so far as they can be regarded as works of art. Actually the various ways of making

1

prints (including photography) are the only methods by which exactly repeatable pictorial statements can be made about anything. The importance of being able exactly to repeat pictorial statements is undoubtedly greater for science, technology, and general information than it is for art.

Historians of art and writers on aesthetic theory have ignored the fact that most of their thought has been based on exactly repeatable pictorial statements about works of art rather than upon first-hand acquaintance with them. Had they paid attention to that fact they might have recognized the extent to which their own thinking and theorizing have been shaped by the limitations imposed on those statements by the graphic techniques. Photography and photographic process, the last of the long succession of such techniques, have been responsible for one of the greatest changes in visual habit and knowledge that has ever taken place, and have led to an almost complete rewriting of the history of art as well as a most thoroughgoing revaluation of the arts of the past.

Although every history of European civilization makes much of the invention in the mid-fifteenth century of ways to print words from movable types, it is customary in those histories to ignore the slightly earlier discovery of ways to print pictures and diagrams. A book, so far as it contains a text, is a container of exactly repeatable word symbols arranged in an exactly repeatable order. Men have been using such containers for at least five thousand years. Because of this it can be argued that the printing of books was no more than a way of making very old and familiar things more cheaply. It may even be said that for a while type printing was little more than a way to do with a much smaller number of proof readings. Prior to 1501 few books were printed in editions larger than that handwritten one of a thousand copies to which Pliny the Younger referred in the second century of our era. The printing of pictures, however, unlike the printing of words from movable types, brought a completely new thing into existence—it made possible for the first time pictorial statements of a kind that could be exactly repeated during the effective life of the printing surface.

This exact repetition of pictorial statements has had incalculable effects upon knowledge and thought, upon science and technology, of every kind. It is hardly too much to say that since the invention of writing there has been no more important invention than that of the exactly repeatable pictorial statement.

Our failure to realize this comes in large measure from the change in the meaning and implications of the word 'print' during the last hundred years. For our great grandfathers, and for their fathers back to the Renaissance, prints were no more and no less than the only exactly repeatable pictorial statements they knew. Before the Renaissance there were no exactly repeatable pictorial statements. Until a century ago, prints made in the old techniques filled all the functions that are now filled by our line cuts and half tones, by our photographs and blueprints, by our various colour processes, and by our political cartoons and pictorial advertisements. If we define prints from the functional point of view so indicated, rather than by any restriction of process or aesthetic value, it becomes obvious that without prints we should have very few of our modern sciences, technologies, archaeologies, or ethnologies—for all of these are dependent, first or last, upon information conveyed by exactly repeatable visual or pictorial statements.

This means that, far from being merely minor works of art, prints are among the most important and powerful tools of modern life and thought. Certainly we cannot hope to realize their actual role unless we get away from the snobbery of modern print collecting notions and definitions and begin to think of them as exactly repeatable pictorial statements or communications, without regard to the accident of rarity or what for the moment we may regard as aesthetic merit. We must look at them from the point of view of general ideas and particular functions, and, especially, we must think about the limitations which their techniques have imposed on them as conveyors of information and on us as receivers of that information.

From very ancient times materials suitable for the making of prints have been available, and apposite skills and crafts have been familiar, but they were not brought into conjunction for the making of exactly repeatable pictorial statements in Europe until roughly about A.D. 1400. In view of this it is worth while to try to think about the situation as it was before there were any prints.

As it seems to be the usual custom to begin with the ancient Greeks when discussing anything that has to do with culture, I shall follow the precedent. There is no possible doubt about the intelligence, the curiosity, and the mental agility of a few of the old Greeks. Neither can there be any doubt about the greatness of their influence on subsequent European culture, even though for the last five hundred years the world has been in active revolt against Greek ideas and ideals. For a very long time we have been taught that after the Greeks there came long periods in which men were not so intelligent as the Greeks had been, and that it was not until the Renaissance that the so intelligent Greek point of view was to some extent recovered. I believe that this teaching, like its general acceptance, has come about because people have confused their ideas of what constitutes intelligence with their ideas about what they have thought of, in the Arnoldian sense, as culture. Culture and intelligence are quite different things. In actual life, people who exemplify Arnoldian culture are no more intelligent than other people, and they have very rarely been among the great creators, the discoverers of new ideas, or the leaders towards social enlightenment. Most of what we think of as culture is little more than the unquestioning acceptance of standardized values.

Historians until very recent times have been literary men and philologues. As students of the past they have rarely found anything they were not looking for. They have been so full of wonder at what the Greeks said, that they have paid little attention to what the Greeks did not do or know. They have been so full of horror at what the Dark Ages did not say, that they have paid no attention to what they did do and know. Modern research, by men who are aware of low subjects like economics and technology, is rapidly

1. Painted woodcut from Boner's *Der Edelstein*, Bamberg, 1461.
About actual size.

2. Metal cut of St. Martin. Reduced.

changing our ideas about these matters. In the Dark Ages, to use their traditional name, there was little assured leisure for pursuit of the niceties of literature, art, philosophy, and theoretical science, but many people, nevertheless, addressed their perfectly good minds to social, agricultural, and mechanical problems. Moreover, all through those academically debased centuries, so far from there having been any falling off in mechanical ability, there was an unbroken series of discoveries and inventions that gave the Dark Ages, and after them the Middle Ages, a technology, and, therefore, a logic, that in many most important respects far surpassed anything that had been known to the Greeks or to the Romans of the Western Empire.

As to the notorious degradation of the Dark Ages, it is to be remembered that during them Byzantium was an integral part of Europe and actually its great political centre of gravity. There was no iron curtain between the East and the West. Intercourse between them was constant and unbroken, and for long periods Byzantium was in actual control of large parts of Italy. We forget the meaning of the word Romagna, and of the Byzantine arts of Venice and South Italy. These things should be borne in mind in view of the silent implication that Byzantium, from which later on so much of Greek learning came to the West, never lost that learning. This implication is probably quite an untrue one. Both East and West saw a great decline in letters. The Academy at Athens was closed in A.D. 529. At Byzantium the university was abolished in the first half of the eighth century. Psellos said that in the reign of the Emperor Romanos (1028–34) the learned at Constantinople had not reached further than the portals of Aristotle and only knew by rote a few catch words of Platonism. The Emperor Constantine (1042–54) revived the university on a small scale and made Psellos its first professor of philosophy. Psellos taught Platonism, which he personally preferred to the then reigning variety of Aristotelianism. So far as concerned intellectual activity there was probably much more in the West than in the East, though directed at such different ends that it evaded the

5

attention of students trained in the traditional classical lore. Where the East let so much of the inherited culture as it retained become gradually static and dull, the West turned from it and addressed its intelligence to new values and new things.

In spite of all this it was the Dark Ages that transmitted to us practically all we have of Greek and Roman literature, science, and philosophy. If the Dark Ages had not to a certain extent been interested in such things it is probable that we should have very little of the classical literatures. People who laboriously copy out by hand the works of Plato and Archimedes, Lucretius and Cicero, Plotinus and Augustine, cannot be accused of being completely devoid of so-called intellectual interests. We forget that the Greeks themselves had forgotten much of their mathematics before the Dark Ages began, and it is easy to overlook such a thinker as Berengar, in the West, who, about the middle of the eleventh century, challenged much of what we regard as Greek thought by asserting that there is no substance in matter aside from the accidents.

The intelligence, as distinct from the culture, of the Dark and Middle Ages, is shown by the fact that in addition to forging the political foundations of modern Europe and giving it a new faith and morality, those Ages developed a great many of what today are among the most basic processes and devices. The Greeks and Romans had no thought of labour-saving devices and valued machinery principally for its use in war—just as was the case in the Old South of the United States, and for much the same reasons. To see this, all one has to do is to read the tenth book of Vitruvius. The Dark and Middle Ages in their poverty and necessity produced the first great crop of Yankee ingenuity.

The breakdown of the Western Empire and the breakdown of its power plant were intimately related to each other. The Romans not only inherited all the Greek technology but added to it, and they passed all this technology on to the Dark Ages. It consisted principally in the manual dexterity and the brute animal force of human beings, most of them in bondage. In the objects that have come down to us from classical times there is little evidence of any actively working and spreading mechanical ingenuity. As shown by Stonehenge, the moving and placement of heavy stones goes back of the beginnings of written history. The Romans did not, however, pass on to the Dark Ages in the West the constantly renewed supply of slaves that constituted the power plant about which the predatory Empire was built. In other words, the Dark Ages found themselves stranded with no power plant and with no tradition or culture of mechanical ingenuity that might provide another power plant of another kind. They had to start from scratch. The real wonder, under all the circumstances, is not that they did so badly but that they did so well.

The great task of the Dark and the Middle Ages was to build for a culture of techniques and technologies. We are apt to forget that it takes much longer to do this than it does to build up a culture of art and philosophy, one reason for this being that the creation of a culture of technologies requires much harder and more accurate thinking. Emotion plays a surprisingly small part in the design and operation of machines and processes, and, curiously, you cannot make a machine work by flogging it. When the Middle Ages had finally produced the roller press, the platen press, and the type-casting mould, they had created the basic tools for modern times.

We have for so long been told about the philosophy, art, and literature, of classical antiquity, and have put them on such a pedestal for worship, that we have failed to observe the patent fact that philosophy, art, and literature can flourish in what are technologically very primitive societies, and that the classical peoples were actually in many ways of the greatest importance not only very ignorant but very unprogressive. Progress and improvement were not classical ideals. The trend of classical thought was to the effect that the past was better than the present and that the story of human existence was one of constant degradation. In spite of all the romantic talk about the joy and serenity of the Greek point of view, Greek thought actually developed into a deeply dyed pessimism that coloured and hampered all classical activities.

7

INTRODUCTION

It is, therefore, worth while to give a short list of some of the things the Greeks and Romans did not know, and that the Middle Ages did know. For most of the examples I shall cite I am indebted to Lynn White's remarkable essay on Technology and Invention in the Middle Ages.[1] The classical Greeks and Romans, although horsemen, had no stirrups. Neither did they think to shoe the hooves of their animals with plates of metal nailed to them. Until the ninth or tenth centuries of our era horses were so harnessed that they pushed against straps that ran high about their necks in such a way that if they threw their weight and strength into their work they strangled themselves. Neither did the classical peoples know how to harness draft animals in front of each other so that large teams could be used to pull great weights. Men were the only animals the ancients had that could pull efficiently. They did not even have wheelbarrows. They made little or no use of rotary motion and had no cranks by which to turn rotary and reciprocating motion into each other. They had no windmills. Such water wheels as they had came late and far between. The classical Greeks and Romans, unlike the Middle Ages, had no horse collars, no spectacles, no algebra, no gunpowder, no compass, no cast iron, no paper, no deep ploughs, no spinning wheels, no methods of distillation, no place value number systems—think of trying to extract a square root with either the Greek or the Roman system of numerals!

The engineers who, in the sixth century A.D., brought the great monolith that caps the tomb of Theodoric across the Adriatic and set it in place, were in no way inferior to the Greek and Roman engineers. The twelfth-century cathedrals of France represent a knowledge of engineering, of stresses and strains, and a mechanical ingenuity far beyond anything dreamed of in classical times. The Athenian Parthenon, no matter what its aesthetic qualities, was but child's play as engineering compared to buildings like the cathedrals at Rheims and Amiens.

It is perhaps hard for us, who have been educated in the fag

[1] *Speculum*, vol. XV, p. 141 (April 1940).

end of the traditional humanistic worship of the classical peoples, to realize that what happened in the ninth and tenth centuries of our era in North-Western Europe was an economic revolution based on animal power and mechanical ingenuity which may be likened to that based on steam power which took place in the late eighteenth and early nineteenth centuries. It shifted the economic and political centre of gravity away from the Mediterranean with its technological ineptitude to the north-west, where it has been ever since. This shift may be said to have had its first official recognition in the two captures of Constantinople in 1203 and 1204. It is customary from the philological point of view to regard these captures as a horrible catastrophe to light and learning, but in fact they actually led to the wiping out of the most influential centre of unprogressive backward-looking traditionalism there was in Europe.

In view of the things the Greeks and Romans did not know, it is possible that the real reason for the so-called darkness of the Dark Ages was the simple fact that they were still in so many ways so very classical.

It is well to remember things of this kind when we are told about the charm of life in Periclean Athens or in the Rome of the Antonines, and how superior it was to that of all the ages that have succeeded them. The inescapable facts are that the Greek and Roman civilizations were based on slavery of the most degrading kind, that slaves did not reproduce themselves, that the supply was only maintained by capture in predatory warfare, and that slavery is incompatible with the creation of a highly developed technology. Although a few of the highly educated Greeks went in for pure mathematics and theoretical science, neither they nor the educated Romans ever lowered themselves to banausic pursuits. They never thought of doing laborious, mechanical things more efficiently or with less human pain and anguish—unless they were captured and sold into slavery, and what they thought then did not matter. As all these things in the end are of great ethical importance, it should also be remembered that the so cultured Greeks left it to the brutal

9

Romans to discover the idea of humanity, and that it was not until the second century of our era that the idea of personality was first given expression. If the educated Greeks and Romans had demeaned themselves by going in for civil technology as hard as they did for a number of other things the story might have been different. But they did not, even in matters that would have been greatly to the advantage of the governing groups in society.

Thus, the Romans are famous for the military roads they built all over the Empire, and the Dark and Middle Ages are held up to scorn for having let those roads go to pieces. However, if we think that those roads were not constructed for civil traffic but as part of the machinery of ruthless military domination of subject peoples, it is possible to regard their neglect as a betterment. Those later Ages substituted other kinds of roads for the Roman variety, roads that were not paved with cemented slabs of stone for the quicker movement of the slogging legions, but roads that, if paved at all, were paved with cobbles, which in many ways and from many unmilitary points of view were more efficient. It is significant that the world has never gone back to the Roman methods of road-building, and that as late as the days of my own youth streets in both London and New York were still paved with cobbles.

To take another example: the Greeks were great seamen. The Athenian Empire was a maritime empire. But the Greeks rowed and did not sail. If you cannot beat up into the wind you cannot sail. All the Greeks' sails enabled them to do was to blow down the wind a little faster. They did not dare to venture beyond sight of land. The rudder at the end of the keel and the lateen and fore and aft sails, like the mariner's compass, were acquisitions of the Dark and Middle Ages. Actually, until the Renaissance and even later, the Mediterranean peoples never learned how to do what we call sailing. The Battle of Lepanto, in 1571, was fought by men in row-boats—large row-boats, to be sure—which grappled with each other so that their men could fight it out hand to hand. The test as between the thought based on the ancient row-boat techniques and that based on the mediaeval deep-water sailing came seventeen years after Lepanto, when the great Spanish Armada met the little English fleet. This was the crucial battle in the last long-drawn-out attempt of the Mediterranean to recover the hegemony it had lost before the end of the tenth century, and in it it went down to utter and disastrous defeat. Within a little more than a hundred years it was distant England that held Gibraltar and Port Mahon and was the great Mediterranean sea power.

On the intellectual and administrative side of ancient life we meet the same lack of mechanical ingenuity. Few people have been more given to books and reading than the upper classes of Greece and Rome. Books were made by copying by hand. The trade in them flourished at Athens, at Alexandria, and at Rome. Great libraries were formed in the Hellenistic period and in the early centuries of the Roman Empire. Plato says that in his time a copy of Anaxagoras could be bought for a drachma, which, according to the Oxford Dictionary, may be considered as being worth less than twenty-five cents. Pliny, the Younger, in the second century of our era, refers to an edition of a thousand copies of a text. Had the Romans had any mechanical way of multiplying the texts of their laws and their legal and administrative rulings and all the forms needed for taxation and other such things, an infinite amount of time and expense would have been saved. But I cannot recall that I have either read or heard of any attempt by an ancient to produce a book or legal form by mechanical means.

In its way the failure of the ancients to address their minds to problems of the kinds I have indicated is one of the most cogent criticisms that can be made of the kind of thought in which they excelled and of its great limitations. The Greeks were full of all sorts of ideas about all sorts of things, but they rarely checked their thought by experiment and they exhibited little interest in discovering and inventing ways to do things that had been un-known to their ancestors. They refined on ancient processes, and in the Hellenistic period they invented ingenious mechanical toys, but it is difficult to point to any technological or labour-saving

11

devices invented by them that were of any momentous social or economic importance. This is shown in several odd ways. For one, the learned writers of accounts of daily life in ancient times have no hesitancy in mixing up details taken from sources that are generations apart, as though they all related to one unchanging state of affairs. For another, modern students have not hesitated to play up as a great and profound virtue the lack of initiative of the Greek craftsmen in looking for new subjects and new manners of work. Thus Percy Gardner, lauding the Greek architects and stone-cutters, in his article on Greek Art in the eleventh edition of the *Encyclopaedia Britannica*, says, 'Instead of trying to invent new schemes, the mason contents himself with improving the regular patterns until they approach perfection.' One can hear the unction drip from that deadly word 'perfection'—one of the greatest inhibitors of intelligent thought that is known to man. The one epoch-making discovery in architectural construction that was made by the classical peoples seems to have been the arch—but the Romans had to bring it with them to Byzantium. Apparently there were no Greek voussoirs, i.e. stones so cut and shaped as to fit together in an arch or vault.

Learned men have devoted many large and expensive volumes to the gathering together of all the literary evidence there is about classical painting and drawing and to the reproduction of all the specimens of such drawing and painting as have been found. It appears from these books that there are no surviving classical pictorial statements, except such as were made incidentally in the decoration of objects and wall surfaces. For such purposes as those there was no need or call for methods to exactly repeat pictorial statements. From the point of view of art as expression or decoration there is no such need, but from that of general knowledge, science, and technology, there is a vast need for them. The lack of some way of producing such statements was no less than a road block in the way of technological and scientific thought and accomplishment.

Lest it be thought that in saying this I am merely expressing a

3. 'The Duchess'. Wood blocks from Holbein's *Dance of Death*,
c. 1520. About actual size, and enlarged head.

4. Woodcut from Osatus's *La vera perfettione del desegno*, Venice 1561.
Slightly enlarged.

personal prejudice, I shall call your attention to what was said about it by a very great and unusually intelligent Roman gentleman, whose writings are held in particularly high esteem by all students of classical times. Some passages in the *Natural History* of Pliny the Elder, a book that was written in the first century of our era, tell the story in the most explicit and circumstantial of manners. As pointed out by Pliny, the Greeks were actually aware of the road block from which they suffered, but far from doing anything about it they accommodated themselves to it by falling back into what can only be called a known and accepted incompetence. More than that, I believe, they built a good deal of their philosophy about this incompetence of theirs. In any case, what happened affords a very apposite example of how life works under the double burden of a pessimistic philosophy and a slave economy. There is nothing more basically optimistic than a new and unprecedented contrivance, even though it be a lethal weapon.

Pliny's testimony is peculiarly valuable because he was an intelligent eye-witness about a condition for which, unfortunately, all the physical evidence has vanished. He cannot have been the only man of his time to be aware of the situation and the call that it made for ingenuity. Seemingly his statement has received but slight attention from the students of the past. This is probably due to the fact that those students had their lines of interest laid down for them before the economic revolution that came to England in the late eighteenth and early nineteenth centuries and did not reach Germany until after 1870, at a time when the learned and the gentry knew nothing and cared less about what they regarded as merely mechanical things. The preoccupation of the post-mediaeval schools and universities with classical thought and literature was probably the greatest of all the handicaps to technological and therefore to social advance. It would be interesting to see a chronological list of the establishments of the first professorships of engineering. With rare exceptions the mechanical callings and knowledges were in the past as completely foreign to the thought and life of the students of ancient times as they were to the young elegants who attended the Academy or walked and talked with Aristotle. So far as I have been able to observe they still are.

In any event, according to Bohn, what Pliny said was this:

'In addition to these (Latin writers), there are some Greek writers who have treated of this subject (i.e. botany). . . . Among these, Crateuas, Dionysius, and Metrodorus, adopted a very attractive method of description, though one which has done little more than prove the remarkable difficulties which attended it. It was their plan to delineate the various plants in colours, and then to add in writing a description of the properties which they possessed. Pictures, however, are very apt to mislead, and more particularly where such a number of tints is required for the imitation of nature with any success; in addition to which, the diversity of copyists from the original paintings, and their comparative degrees of skill, add very considerably to the chances of losing the necessary degree of resemblance to the originals . . .' (Chap. 4, Book 25).

'Hence it is that other writers have confined themselves to a verbal description of the plants; indeed some of them have not so much as described them even, but have contented themselves for the most part with a bare recital of their names, considering it sufficient if they pointed out their virtues and properties to such as might feel inclined to make further inquiries into the subject' (Chap. 5, Book 25).

'The plant known as "paeonia" is the most ancient of them all. It still retains the name of him who was the first to discover it, being known also as the "pentorobus" by some, and the "glyciside" by others; indeed this is one of the great difficulties attendant on forming an accurate knowledge of plants, that the same object had different names in different districts' (Chap. 10, Book 25).[1]

It is to be noted that in his account of the breakdown of Greek botany, Pliny does not fall back upon general ideas of a woolly

[1] Quoted by permission of G. Bell & Sons, Ltd., the present publishers of Bohn's Library.

kind. There is no Zeitgeist explanation, no historicism, no sugges-
tion that things were not done simply because people in their
wisdom and good taste preferred not to do them even though of
course they could have done them if they had wanted to. Pliny's
reason is as hard and brutal a fact as a bridge that has collapsed
while being built. This essay amounts to little more than a summary account of the long slow discovery of ways to erect that
bridge.

In view of this I shall rephrase what Pliny said: The Greek
botanists realized the necessity of visual statements to give their
verbal statements intelligibility. They tried to use pictures for the
purpose, but their only ways of making pictures were such that
they were utterly unable to repeat their visual statements wholly
and exactly. The result was such a distortion at the hands of the
successive copyists that the copies became not a help but an
obstacle to the clarification and the making precise of their verbal
descriptions. And so the Greek botanists gave up trying to use
illustrations in their treatises and tried to get along as best they
could with words. But, with words alone, they were unable to
describe their plants in such a way that they could be recognized—
for the same things bore different names in different places and the
same names meant different things in different places. So, finally,
the Greek botanists gave up even trying to describe their plants
in words, and contented themselves by giving all the names they
knew for each plant and then told what human ailments it was
good for. In other words, there was a complete breakdown of
scientific description and analysis once it was confined to words
without demonstrative pictures.

What was true of botany as a science of classification and
recognition of plants was also true of an infinite number of other
subjects of the very greatest importance and interest to men. Common nouns and adjectives, which are the materials with which a
verbal description is made, are after all only the names of vaguely
described classes of things of the most indefinite kind and without
precise concrete meanings, unless they can be exemplified by

pointing to actual specimens. In the absence of actual specimens the best way (perhaps the only way) of pointing is by exhibiting properly made pictures. We can get some idea of this by trying to think what a descriptive botany or anatomy, or a book on machines or on knots and rigging, or even a sempstress's handbook, would be like in the absence of dependable illustrations. The only knowledges in which the Greeks made great advances were geometry and astronomy, for the first of which words amply suffice, and for the second of which every clear night provides the necessary invariant image to all the world.

All kinds of reasons have been alleged in explanation of the slow progress of science and technology in ancient times and in the ages that succeeded them, but no reference is ever made to the deterrent effect of the lack of any way of precisely and accurately repeating pictorial statements about things observed and about tools and their uses. The revolutionary techniques that filled this lack first came into general use in the fifteenth century. Although we can take it for granted that the making of printed pictures began some time about 1400, recognition of the social, economic, and scientific, importance of the exact repetition of pictorial statements did not come about until long after printed pictures were in common use. This is shown by the lateness of most of the technical illustrated accounts of the techniques of making things. As examples I may cite the first accounts of the mechanical methods of making exactly repeatable statements themselves. Thus the first competent description of the tools and technique of etching and engraving was the little book that Abraham Bosse published in 1645; the first technical account of the tools and processes used in making types and printing from them was that published by Joseph Moxon in 1683; and the first similar account of woodcutting, the oldest of all these techniques, was the *Traité* of J. M. Papillon, which bears on its title page the date 1766. It is not impossible that Moxon's *Mechanick Exercises*, which were published serially in the last years of the seventeenth century, had much to do with England's early start in the industrial revolution.

Anyone who is gifted with the least mechanical ingenuity can understand these books and go and do likewise. But he can do so only because they are filled with pictures of the special tools used and of the methods of using them. Parts of Moxon's account of printing can be regarded as studies in the economy of motion in manipulation. I have not run the matter down, but I should not be surprised if his book were not almost the first in which such things were discussed.

Of many of the technologies and crafts requiring particular manual skills and the use of specialized tools there seem to have been no adequate accounts until the completion of the great and well illustrated *Encyclopaedia* of Diderot and his fellows in the third quarter of the eighteenth century, just before the outbreak of the French Revolution. But the *Encyclopaedia* was a very expensive and very large set of volumes, intended for and limited to the use of the rich. Curiously, the importance of its contribution to a knowledge of the arts and crafts has attracted comparatively little attention as compared to that which has been given to its articles on political matters, although there is good reason to think that they had equally great results.

The last century is still so close to us and we are so busy keeping up with the present one, that it is hard for us to realize the meaning of the fact that the last hundred and fifty years have seen the greatest and most thoroughgoing revolution in technology and science that has ever taken place in so short a time. In western Europe and in America the social, as well as the mechanical, structure of society and life has been completely refashioned. The late Professor Whitehead made the remarkable observation that the greatest invention of the nineteenth century was that of the technique of making inventions. But he did not point out that this remarkable invention was based in very large measure on that century's sudden realization that techniques and technologies can only be effectively described by written or printed words when they are accompanied by adequate demonstrative pictures.

The typical eighteenth-century methods of book illustration

were engraving and etching. Etchings and engravings have always been expensive to make and to use as book illustrations. The books that were fully illustrated with them were, with few exceptions, intended for the consumption of the rich and the traditionally educated classes. In the eighteenth century the title pages of these books sometimes described them as being 'adorned with elegant sculptures', or other similar words. The words 'adorned' and 'elegant' tell the story of their limitations, mental and financial alike. Lest it be thought that the phrase I have just quoted came from some polite book of verse or essays, I may say that it has stuck in my memory ever since at the age of ten I saw it on the title page of a terrifying early eighteenth-century edition of *Foxe's Martyrs*, in which the illustrators went all out to show just what happened to the Maryian heretics. Under the circumstances I can think of few phrases that throw more light on certain aspects of eighteenth-century life and thought.

Although hundreds of thousands of legible impressions could be printed at low cost from the old knife-made woodcuts, the technique of woodcutting was not only out of fashion in the eighteenth century, but its lines were too coarse and the available paper was too rough for the woodcut to convey more than slight information of detail and none of texture.

At the end of the eighteenth century and the beginning of the nineteenth century a number of very remarkable inventions were made. I shall mention but three of them. First, Bewick, in the 1780's, developed the technique of using an engravers, tool on the end of the wood, so that it became possible to produce from a wood-block very fine lines and delicately gradated tints, provided it were printed on smooth and not too hard paper. Next, in 1798, Robert, in France, invented, and shortly afterwards, in England, Fourdrinier perfected, a paper-making machine, operated by power, either water or steam, which produced paper by a continuous process. It also made possible the production of paper with a wove surface that was smoother than any that had previously been made in Europe. When fitted with calendar rolls the machine produced paper that was so smooth it was shiny. Finally, just before 1815, Koenig, a German resident in England, devised for the (*London*) *Times* a printing press that was operated by power and not by the strength of men's backs. In connection with a revival of Ged's earlier invention of stereotyping, these inventions brought about a very complete revolution in the practice of printing and publishing. The historians of printing have devoted their attention to the making of fine and expensive books, and in so doing they have overlooked the great function of books as conveyors of information. The history of the cheap illustrated book and its role in the self-education of the multitude has yet to be written.

It took but a comparatively short time for these three or four inventions to spread through the world. As they became familiar there was such a flood of cheap illustrated informative books as had never before been known. Nothing even approaching it had been seen since the sixteenth century. It took only a few decades for the publishers everywhere to begin turning out books of this kind at very low prices. In a short time the world ceased to talk about the 'art and mystery' of its crafts. In France they said that the Revolutionary law abolishing the guilds opened the careers to the talents, but it was actually these cheap illustrated informative books that opened the crafts to everyone, no matter how poor or unlearned, provided only that he knew how to read and to understand simple pictures. As examples of this I may cite the well-known *Manuels Roret*, the publication of which goes back to 1825, and the English *Penny Cyclopaedia* which began in 1833. It is to be noted that for a long time in the nineteenth century the upper classes and the traditionally educated made few contributions to the rapidly lengthening list of new inventions, and that so many of those inventions were made by what in England until very recent years were condescendingly referred to as 'self-educated men'. The fact was that the classicizing education of the men who were not self educated prevented them from making inventions.

In the Renaissance they had found a solution of the dilemma

19

of the Greek botanists as described by Pliny. In the nineteenth century informative books usefully illustrated with accurately repeatable pictorial statements became available to the mass of mankind in western Europe and in America. The result was the greatest revolution in practical thought and accomplishment that has ever been known. This revolution was a matter as momentous from the ethical and political points of view as from the mechanical and economic ones. The masses had begun to get the one great tool they most needed to enable them to solve their own problems. Today the news counters in our smallest towns are piled with cheap illustrated magazines at which the self-consciously educated turn up their noses, but in those piles are prominently displayed long series of magazines devoted to mechanical problems and ways of doing things, and it would be well for the cultured if they but thought a little about the meaning of that.

I think it can be truthfully said that in 1800 no man anywhere, no matter how rich or highly placed, lived in such physical comfort or so healthily, or enjoyed such freedom of mind and body, as do the mechanics of today in my little Connecticut town.

If any one thing can be credited with this it is the pervasion of the cheap usefully informative illustrated book.

# II

# THE ROAD BLOCK BROKEN

# THE FIFTEENTH CENTURY

PRINTS began to pervade the life and thought of western Europe in the fifteenth century. It is therefore necessary to take a glance at what we have been told about that century.

Probably the worst way there is to discover the most important thing done in any historic period is to take the word of that period for it. What to the generation of its occurrence is merely a casual happening, an amusing toy, or an impractical intellectual or physical adventure, in time frequently becomes all-important for the world.

In spite of this we are still asked to think of the Renaissance in terms of what some literary people of that time thought were the most important things it did. Thus almost every book dealing with the Renaissance says that the principal events of the fifteenth century were the recoveries of Greek thought and of the classical forms of art. This statement is so customary and is made with such an air of finality that most of us have come to believe it. And, yet, on the very face of the record, it is impossible to believe it. We have forgotten that the literary and artistic men who evolved and

21

told us this fairy tale were much more ignorant of the Middle Ages, and even of the Renaissance itself, than the Middle Ages were ignorant of Greek thought.

In the first place, what is called Greek thought is not a homogeneous body of doctrine and knowledge reflecting a reasoned and unified attitude towards life and the world. What remains of it is a highly accidental heap of notions and odds and ends of the most violently contradictory kinds. If you care to look for it you can find a phrase in it that can be twisted to the purpose of almost anything you want to argue on any side of any problem. The Greeks never agreed about anything; they actually knew very little; it was quite customary for them to be intellectually dishonest; their arguments were designed, not to bring out the truth, but to down the other fellow in a forensic victory; and they had very loose and careless tongues. Although we are always told that Aristotle discovered logic, it should be obvious that no one man could possibly have been its discoverer. Much of Aristotle's teaching was very illogical, and on the whole it undoubtedly hampered subsequent thought much more than it helped it.

In the second place, it is easy to forget that many of the scholastic doctrines and modes of thought which had dominated much of mediaeval thinking were specifically Aristotelian, which is to say that they were Greek. The shift away from scholasticism was not so much the result of any discovery of Greek thought as a revulsion from it. That this shift took the initial form of a limited and superficial fashion for neo-Platonism and for the exterior nudity, though not for the interior content, of Roman art, can be regarded as little more than a passing phase of the basic revolt. However important it may have seemed to certain restricted and loquacious portions of Renaissance society, this fashion in itself made singularly little difference to the part of the world that was beginning to think new thoughts and to do new things.

Contrary to what we have long been taught, the effective thinking of the Renaissance was not merely a resurrection of classical ideas. As we can see it today, the really great event of

22

the Renaissance was the emergence of attitudes, and kinds and objects of thought that were neither Aristotelian nor Platonic, nor yet Greek at all, but in so far as they had never attracted the attention of the writers and literary men, quite new and different. To a great extent they were the results of materials and technological problems completely unknown to the ancient world. What actually happened in the fifteenth century was the effective beginning of that practical struggle for liberation from the trammels of Greek ideas which has been the outstanding characteristic of the last five hundred years.

Passing over what the inventors, the technicians, the explorers, and the statesmen did, several events happened in the first half of the fifteenth century that are not given their due prominence in the standard accounts of the period. One of these was the pervasion of ways of making printed pictures—in other words of making exactly repeatable pictorial statements. Another was Leon Battista Alberti's enunciation, in 1435, of a method of perspective drawing, which, whether or not he or his contemporaries knew it, provided a geometrical rationalization for pictorial statements of space relationships, that was eventually to develop into a basic geometry or mathematics of a qualitative as distinct from the quantitative Greek kind. Perspective rapidly became an essential part of the technique of making informative pictures, and before long was demanded of pictures that were not informative. Its introduction had much to do with that western European preoccupation with verisimilitude, which is probably the distinguishing mark of subsequent European picture making. The third of these events was Nicholas of Cusa's enunciation, in 1440, of the first thoroughgoing doctrines of the relativity of knowledge and of the continuity, through transitions and middle terms, between extremes. This was a fundamental challenge to definitions and ideas that had tangled thought since the time of the ancient Greeks.

These things, the exactly repeatable pictorial statement, a logical grammar for representation of space relationships in pictorial statements, and the concepts of relativity and continuity, were and still are superficially so unrelated that they are rarely thought of seriously in conjunction with one another. But, between them, they have revolutionized both the descriptive sciences and the mathematics on which the science of physics rests, and in addition they are essential to a great deal of modern technology. Their effects on art have been very marked. They were absolutely new things in the world. There was no precedent for them in classical practice or thought of any kind or variety.

Now—I shall try to sketch the outlines of the development of the printed picture during the fifteenth and sixteenth centuries. In doing this I propose to regard artistic merit as a matter of subsidiary importance, and to look at the evidence from the point of view of that communication of visual information and ideas which, for the last four centuries, has been the primary function of the exactly repeatable pictorial statement.

No one knows when or where in western Europe men first began to print designs and pictures from wood-blocks and metal plates. To save time and to avoid getting lost in a discussion of detail that, however fascinating, is of little importance, I may sum up the story by saying there is reason to believe that woodcuts were made before engravings were, and that both were made before etchings were. The extant evidence enables us to guess that in 1400 there were very few if any prints in Europe. The evidence also enables us to know that by the middle of the fifteenth century the making of woodcuts and engravings was widely practised in a number of European countries, and that before the end of the century etchings were being made in south Germany.

It is generally thought that, as the requisite tools, materials, and skills for the making of woodcuts were to be found in the shops of the painters and carvers, the making of woodcuts began in those shops. Similar reasoning indicates that engraving took its start in the shops of the gold and silver smiths, and etching in those of the armourers.

The most primitive woodcuts we have were rubbings from

5. Portion of a late impression of an early North Italian engraving of St. Jerome. Enlarged.

6. Portion of the engraved Bacchanal with Silenus, by Mantegna (1431-1506). Reduced.

7. The same portion of a pen and ink copy by Dürer. Reduced.

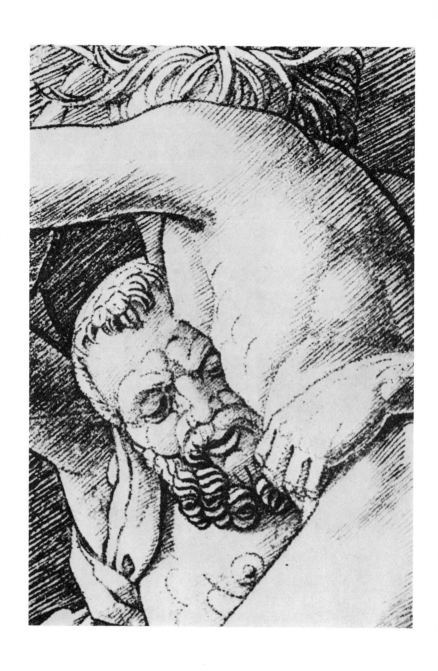

8. Portion of an early Italian engraving after a drawing by Mantegna. Enlarged.

9. Portion of an early fifteenth-century woodcut of St. Christopher.
About actual size.

wood-blocks and were not struck off in a press. The use of the printing press undoubtedly was known to the makers of woodcuts at least as early, if not earlier, than it was to the printers from movable types. The earliest known picture of a printing press for type or woodcuts is said to be that contained in the Lyonese *Dance of Death* of 1499. There is no technical description of one until

10. The earliest picture of a printing press. Woodcut from a *Dance of Death,* Lyons, 1499. Reduced.

almost two hundred years later. How the earliest engravings were printed is not known, but it was probably by some method of rubbing or burnishing—a method still used in goldsmiths' and gun-smiths' shops. When the roller press came into use is not known, but it was presumably some time in the middle years of the fifteenth century.

The dated prints prior to 1460 are so few in number and of such widely diverse characteristics that it is impossible to use them as evidence for the dating of the undated prints. They do not form an integrated series. Prints of advanced and primitive technical types have always been made simultaneously, just as they are at the present time. Because of this the history of prints does not leave the realm of conjecture and hazardous connoisseurship until the first use of woodcuts as illustrations in books printed from movable types, a very large and useful number of which are either definitely dated or datable with some approximate degree of accuracy within a short period of years. After about 1460 the history of the woodcut is known to us by a long and closely integrated series of dated and closely datable documents. It is perhaps worth while to mention, in passing, that after that time the fifteenth-century woodcuts in books are in general much more interesting as works of art than are the single-sheet woodcuts.

The earliest book printed from type to contain woodcuts is said to be the *Edelstein* of Ulrich Boner, which was printed at Bamberg by Ulrich Pfister, a church dignitary and amateur printer who seems to have had no relations with Gutenberg and his circle. Pfister produced two different editions of the *Edelstein* with the same illustrations, one of them undated, the other dated 1461. It is interesting to notice that this is eleven years earlier than the date in the earliest known dated block-book.

The integrated series of engravings does not begin until somewhat later. The use of engravings for book illustrations was rare and sporadic until about the middle of the fifteen-hundreds. We have rough ideas about when many of the early engravers worked, but their prints are rarely dated and it is impossible to arrange their prints in time orders, let alone in chronological lists.

A small number of the earliest types of single-sheet woodcuts were merely patterned papers to be pasted on boxes and other objects as decoration. Some of the earliest types are to be found on playing-cards. But most of the early single-sheet woodcuts were of religious subjects. The same things are true in general of the earliest engravings, with the remarkable exception that quite a number of pattern designs for the use of gold- and silversmiths are to be found among them. These pattern designs seem to be the

27

first exactly repeatable pictorial statements that were intended to provide ideas or information that could be put to work.

The subject matter of a print, like its purpose and the social group at which it is directed, has always had a great deal to do with how it is made. We see this even today in the qualitative differences between the pictorial advertisements of the Fifth Avenue merchants and those of the mail order houses. The single-sheet woodcuts seem to have been made for very simple people. The figures in them are no more than class symbols, which stand for some particular saint or such an object of religious veneration as the Vernicle or the Sacred Heart. The identification of the personage represented is accomplished by the use of an attribute or sign that is specially connected with him. Well before the end of the century the cloven hoof of manufacture showed itself in these prints, for there are some that have changeable heads and attributes printed from little blocks dropped into slots left for the purpose in the bigger blocks. Thus different saints would have identical bodies, clothes, backgrounds, and accessories, all printed from one identical block. The people for whom these prints were made obviously looked to them not for information but for the awakening of pious emotions. Doubtless there was a good deal of superstition also, as is indicated by the fact that a great many of these prints represent saints who were prayed to for protection against particular dangers and sicknesses.

That these early prints were not looked to for information is shown in several ways in addition to those that I have mentioned. Thus, the first edition of Schreiber's great catalogue of the fifteenth-century single-sheet woodcuts described only eleven portraits and three views—and all of them were made at the end of the century. I think I am correct in saying that there is no single-sheet woodcut in the Schreiber catalogue that depicts a device or method of doing anything, except in a wholly accidental and incidental manner. Except for the engraved pattern designs, the same thing in general is true of the early engravings.

Another way in which we can see that the informational

capacity of the print was not realized for a long time, is by noting how many of the early woodcuts were daubed up with colour carelessly applied in such a way as to cover and obscure their lines. So far as their buyers were concerned prints were just pictures and not a special kind of pictorial statement that could be exactly repeated. Exact repeatability meant no more to the original purchasers than it does today to the buyers of greeting cards. So far as the maker was concerned a print was merely a picture made by a process which saved time and labour in quantity production. The printing surface from which they were struck off was no more and no less than a capital investment in specialized machinery.

The only material difference between the woodcut and the engraving, so far as concerns things of this kind, was that the engraved plate wore out much faster than the wood-block and was more expensive to make and to print. While the functions of the two were the same, the engraving was, in comparison with the woodcut, an article of luxury. It is to be doubted that either woodcuts or engravings became objects of interest to the great and the wealthy until towards the end of the fifteenth century. Such intellectual interests as they represented were thus distinctly of bourgeois kinds. It may be said that this has in general been true through most of the history of prints.

The early woodcut book illustrations, like the early single-sheet prints, were often daubed up with coarse and careless colour. This practice was far less frequent in Italy than it was in the north. It is not improbable that many of the more popular early picture books were sold 'penny plain, and tuppence coloured', as was the famous *Nuremberg Chronicle* of 1493. The *Schatzbehalter* of 1491 actually contains an instruction for the colouring of one of its pictures. The illustrations of the Pfister books in the 1460's were so painted up that they became merely crude and gaudy decorations of the printed pages.

One of the most curious survivals in thought about the design of picture books is the widely held and expressed notion that illustrations are mere decorations, and that as such no illustrations are 'good' unless, as people say, they 'harmonize' with the printed text pages and do not attract attention to themselves or interfere with the balance of the blocks of type. This procrustean notion flourishes among people who know books only as means for diversion and who think that the way to test the design of a book is to look at it two pages at a time—although no mere human being

11. Woodcut from Torquemada's *Meditationes*, Rome, 1473. Reduced.

can read more than one page or see more than one illustration at a time. This idea was loudly expressed by William Morris and some of the typographical ideologues who followed in his train. The irony of the doctrine can only be fully appreciated when we think that very few of the greatly illustrated books conform to the Morrisanian teaching, while many very poorly illustrated books do.

In the following survey, I regret that I shall be able to mention only a very few of the more notable books. Other persons familiar with the material might easily select quite different examples for comment without in the least changing the general argument.

It was not until 1467, at Rome, that the earliest set of datable prints was issued that purported to be pictures of precisely identifiable and locatable objects. These were the woodcuts in the Cardinal Torquemada's *Meditations on the Passion of Our Lord.* According to the first and the last sentences in the book, they represent pictures with which the Cardinal had decorated his

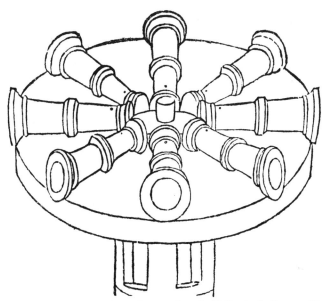

12. A machine gun. Portion of a woodcut in Valturius's *De re militari,* Verona, 1472. Reduced.

titular church of Santa Maria sopra Minerva. As the book was one of edification and not of information, this fact was probably a matter of complete indifference to its readers, but doubtless the Cardinal took great pride in it.

Five years after the appearance of the Torquemada, there appeared at Verona, in 1472, an edition of Valturius's *Art of War,* which was illustrated with many large and small woodcuts specifically representing machinery and its uses. This was not edification at all, and neither was it mere decoration. It was the deliberate communication of information and ideas. The historians have

31

concentrated their interest on some technicalities in the printing of the book and on the identity of the designer of the woodcuts, but they have unanimously overlooked the importance of these

## NOMEN HERBAE ASPARAGI AGRESTIS.

13. 'Asparagus agrestis', woodcut from the herbal of the *Pseudo-Apuleius*, Rome, *c.* 1483. About actual size.

illustrations as the first dated set of illustrations made definitely for informational purposes. Whatever we may think about Valturius's machines from our present-day mechanical point of view, it seems certain that on the whole they represent a very notable

32

14. Head from an early German engraving by the Master E.S. Enlarged.

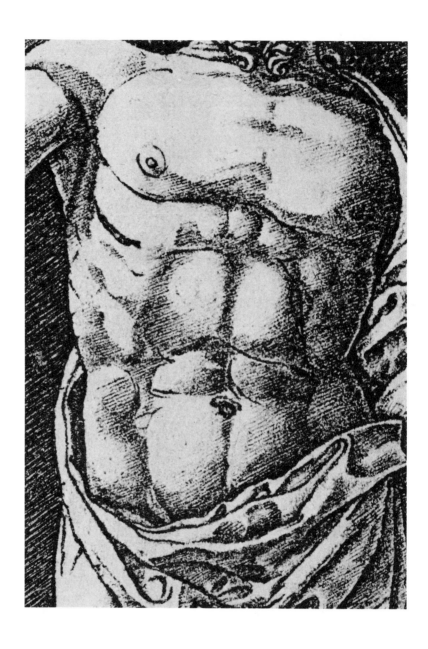

15. Torso from the engraving of The Risen Christ between Saints Andrew and Longinus, by Mantegna. Enlarged.

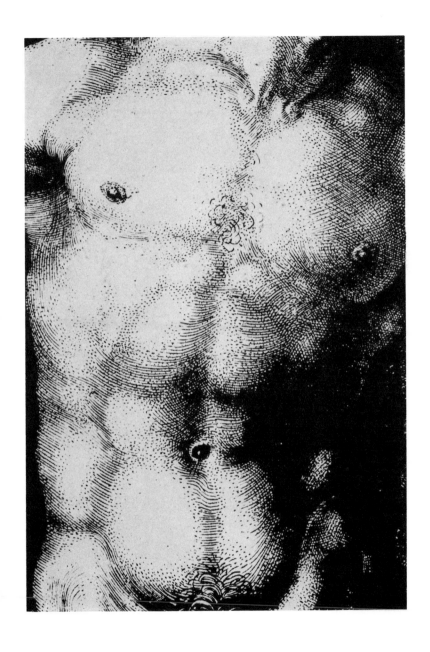

16. Torso from Dürer's engraving of Adam and Eve (1504). Enlarged.

17. Torso from Dürer's woodcut of The Trinity (1511). Enlarged.

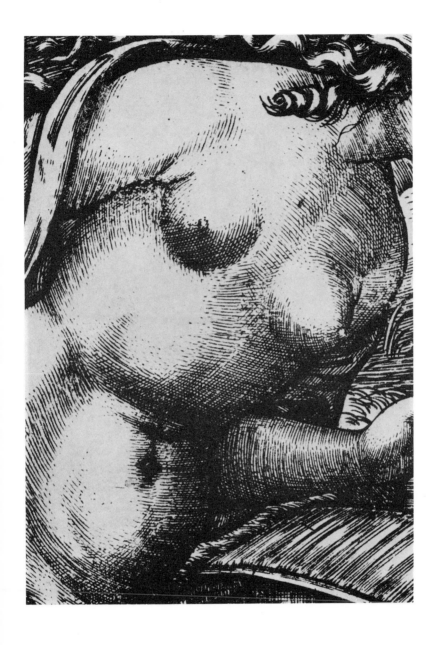

18. Torso from Marc Antonio's early engraving of Pyramus and Thisbe (1505). Enlarged.

19. Portion of Marc Antonio's late engraving of Jupiter and Cupid (c. 1518).
Enlarged.

20. Portion of Lucas of Leyden's engraving of Lot and his daughters (1530).
Enlarged.

21. Portion of an engraving of the Laocoon, published by Lafreri (mid XVI century). Enlarged.

technological advance over the practice of the classical Greeks and Romans. The figures in the cuts are represented in costumer's 'classical' armour, but the things they are doing and the tools they are using are frequently quite unclassical. They provide a very pretty example of the necessity to keep in mind the difference between fancy costume and actuality. We are merely amused by deliberate modern anachronisms of this kind, as when *Hamlet* or *Julius Caesar* is performed in modern clothes, but when Renaissance figures are represented in armour showing 'classical' forms humourless people are only too apt to say that they show the deep influence of classical thought, and to forget that the picture as a whole is a direct denial of that thought and as unclassical as it can possibly be.

In 1475 Konrad von Megenburg's *Book of Nature* was published at Augsburg. It was the first illustrated printed encyclopaedia, but its few illustrations were also encyclopaedic and unlabelled. They can have been of no use to anyone in search of information of a precise kind. A Milanese book of 1479 contains what is said to be the first portrait to appear in a printed book.

Then, some time just after 1480, there was published at Rome the so-called *Pseudo-Apuleius,* a book that contains much for thought. Its text is that of a ninth-century botanical manuscript which for centuries prior to the last war was in the monastery at Subiaco. Its woodcuts are careless copies of the illustrations in that manuscript, but they are actually closer to their originals than we should expect in view of the then prevalent attitude towards such things. They were the final step in a long series of copies of copies of copies that went back to original drawings made not impossibly by some of the Greek botanists of whom Pliny talked. They point the moral of his account of why the Greek botanists gave up trying to illustrate their books. In any case, this was the first illustrated botany book to be printed, and it was also the first printed reproduction of both the text and the illustrations in a very ancient volume. It was the Adam from which sprang that line of facsimiles of old manuscripts and drawings that every museum and university library prides itself in having on its shelves.

In 1484 the herbal known as the *Latin Herbarius* was printed at Mainz. It is a large and fully illustrated volume containing many woodcuts of plants, that seem to have been copied from various older sources. It suffers, though not so badly, from the same trouble as the *Pseudo-Apuleius*. The next year, 1485, however, the same printer issued another and completely different herbal in German, which is known as the *Gart der Gesundheit*. Its handsome and well-drawn illustrations were epoch making in the history of prints as a medium for the conveyance of information in invariant form. It is pleasant to let the author tell the story in his own words. In his brief introduction he says:

'. . . as man has no greater or nobler treasure on this earth than bodily health, I came to believe that I could undertake no more honourable or useful or holier work or labour, than to bring together a book in which the virtue and nature of many herbs and other creations of God, with their true colours and form, were made comprehensible for the consolation and use of all the world. Therefore, I caused this praiseworthy book to be begun by a master learned in medicine, who at my request brought together in a book the virtue and nature of many herbs out of the esteemed masters of medicine, Galen, Avicenna . . . and others. And when I was in the middle of the work of drawing and painting the herbs I noticed that many noble herbs did not grow in this German land, so that, except by hearsay, I could not draw them in their true colours and form. Therefore, I left the work I had begun unfinished and hanging in the pen until I had received grace and dispensation to go to the Holy Sepulchre. . . . And so, lest this noble work, begun but not ended, be left undone, and also that my journey should serve not only the salvation of my soul but all the world, I took with me a painter of understanding and with a subtle and practised hand. And so I travelled. . . . In journeying through these kingdoms and lands I diligently learned the herbs that were

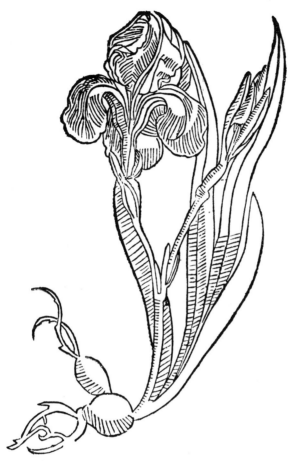

**Gladiolus** notten krut oder geel swertein
Capitulũ·cȝcv· *195*

Ladiolus latine·grece dȝȝeris·Die meifter fprechen
daȝ diß krut haße keynen ftengel vnd hait bletter die
wachfen vfȝ der wurtzeln die glichen eynes fwertes
lamel·vñ ift ȝweyer hande·Eyns wechfet an drucke
fteten vnd hait eyn fqe blomen die ift weych vñ wol

22. 'Gladiolus', woodcut from the *Gart der Gesundheit*, Mainz,
1485  Reduced.

there, and had them painted and drawn in their true colours and form. And afterwards, when, with God's help, I was come again in German land and home, the great love which I had for this work has moved me to finish it. . . . And in order that it may be of use to the learned and the lay I have had it turned into German.'

The *Gart der Gesundheit* is thus the first printed illustrated account of the results of a journey undertaken with scientific purposes in mind. I know of no earlier statement that a writer on a scientific subject refused to have his book illustrated from hearsay and took care that it be done directly from the original objects represented. Because of this it is one of the greatest monuments in the history of the descriptive sciences. It is to be regretted that we know the names neither of the man who undertook the task, of the learned man who assembled the literary material, nor of the subtle artist who made the drawings.

In that same year, 1485, there came out at Venice an illustrated edition of Sacrobosco's *Sphaera Mundi*, a book on astronomy. Its diagrams included one of an eclipse, which is printed, not painted or stencilled, in black, red, and yellow, and is reputed to be the first instance in which three colours were used in a wholly printed picture or diagram. It is thus one of the monuments in the history of the exactly repeatable pictorial statement.

The next year, in 1486, at Mainz, there appeared the first edition of Breydenbach's *Travels*. This was the first illustrated book of travel to come from the press. Its pictures were made by Erhard Rewich of Utrecht, who made the trip with the author. Among them are views of cities, pictures of costumes, and a number of Eastern alphabets. Some of these aphabets had not previously been seen in print. Some of the views are valuable documents about still extant buildings that are represented in them. A number of the large views are printed on folding sheets, that of Venice being about six feet long. It was apparently the first time that such things made their appearance in a printed

23. Portion of a woodcut view of Venice in Breydenbach's *Peregrinationes*, Mainz, 1486. Enlarged.

book. The general attitude of the time towards the difference between first- and second-hand visual information is shown by the fact that Carpaccio, the great Venetian painter, was content, for one of his pictures, to copy from Rewich's view of Venice rather than to draw the buildings directly for himself.

In 1493, a Nuremberg printer, named Hans Mayr, issued illustrated catalogues of the precious objects in the possession of several of the German cathedrals. So far as I know these are the first illustrated printed catalogues of any specific collections of any sort of material.

In the same year, 1493, there was published the famous *Nuremberg Chronicle*, which is still noteworthy for the brute number of woodcut illustrations it contained. There are said to be no less than 1809 of them, but they were printed from a much smaller number of blocks. In addition to pictures of notable events, such as the six days of the creation, and objects like Noah's Ark, there are many portraits and views of cities. Some of these are copied from earlier prints. The portrait of the Sultan, ironically, is a version of Pisanello's medal of the Emperor John Palaeologus. The same heads and views appear with quite different captions in different parts of the book. One view does duty for no less than eleven separate towns. Many of the pictures, however, of German towns and of a few foreign ones, such as those of Venice and Rome, show that some endeavour was made towards at least a slight degree of verisimilitude. The book may perhaps be regarded as the culminating example of the ancient and mediaeval careless attitude towards verisimilitude, though it must be confessed that it has had serious competitors down to the present day. We find these competitors even in our most learned books and best museums, where they parade themselves as restorations of sculpture and models of ancient buildings. They also occur in many of the most advertised re-creations of old buildings, such as those at Williamsburg in Virginia. The classical archaeologists of a generation or so ago were very fond of these flights of imagination, the net result of which was that some observing people came to think it odd that so many of the Greek sculptors and architects spoke such fluent German. But this is a subject that, while it would richly repay investigation, is not popular among the learned.

Looking back at these illustrated informational books of the late fifteenth century we may be inclined to laugh at most of them, but the fact remains that they were quite serious and that the information they conveyed was the best that could be provided by the poor fellows who gave it. If we do laugh at them, and if we also want to be consistent, we must also laugh at the pictures in many of the solemn books I studied when I was a lad, and even at many of those that have appeared during very recent years. The pictures in almost all books on art and archaeology that were printed prior to the time I was born were little more than travesties of the objects they purported to represent. The fifteenth-century illustrations are actually no funnier distortions of fact than those in the edition of Dr. R. C. Lodge's standard translation of Winckelmann's *History of Ancient Art* that was published at Boston in 1880, or for that matter those in the books by Perrot and Chipiez, or by Luebke, or Murray, and ever so many others that I pored over in my childhood and youth.

In passing it is interesting to notice that many of the little pamphlets that came from the Florentine presses during the last decade of the fifteenth century not only were illustrated but were distinctly political in nature. These were not only the first political tracts addressed to a popular audience, but their charming wood-cuts are the first body of printed political cartoons.

In 1504, at Toul, in France, Pelerin published his book on *Perspective*, the first on that subject to reach print, and also the first to teach the modern 'three point' method. Its illustrations are the first to appear in a printed book in which we feel as though we were looking at pictures of rational spaces.

The earliest fully illustrated account of a craft or art that I recall is Fanti's *Theory and Practice of Writing*, that was printed at Venice in 1514. It is a detailed description of the forms of written letters and of the ways of forming them with the pen.

From this time on illustrated books of information came from the presses of Europe with ever increasing profusion and with steadily increasing accuracy of representation. It is impractical here to give an account of even the most important books of this kind that dealt with astronomy and archaeology, anatomy and animals, birds and fishes, machinery and techniques, costumes and clothing, architecture and engineering, and many other subjects, but I should like to call particular attention to several of the botanies, because in a way they typify the whole movement.

The publication of the herbals of 1484 and 1485 was followed by that of many others in many places. For a period of almost fifty years most of these other books were illustrated with copies of the woodcuts in those two herbals, many of which were copied from them at second and even third hand, with a steadily decreasing size in the dimensions of the pictures and a steady increase in the amount of distortion of the representations. The degradation and distortion thus introduced into the pictures perhaps reached their culmination in the first English herbal, the *Grete Herbal*, of 1526, in which the pictures have at last become little more than decorative motifs much more suited to serve as cross stitch patterns than for the conveyance of information. They constitute a remarkably sad example of what happens to visual information as it passes from copyist to copyist.

These herbals, beginning with the *Pseudo-Apuleius* of about 1480 and coming down through the *Grete Herbal* of 1526, are extremely interesting from still another point of view. When arranged in families and in a time order they clearly show the operation of what I suppose is one of the basic human characteristics. So long as the illustrators did not return to the original plants as sources of information about their shapes, but confined themselves to such knowledge of the forms as they could extract from pictures made by earlier men—to what may be called hearsay and not first-hand evidence—it was inevitable that they should rationalize their own pictorial accounts and overlook or disregard what appeared to them to be mere irrationalities in the

24. A Living Room. Woodcut from Pelerin's *De Perspectiva*, Toul, 1504. Reduced.

pictorial accounts given by their predecessors. This rationalization most frequently took the form of an endeavour for symmetry, which produced regular shapes that not only lost all verisimilitude of lines and edges but introduced a balanced arrangement of parts and forms, which, however satisfying to mental habits, resulted in a very complete misrepresentation of the actual facts. I am sure that all sorts of morals can be drawn from these botanical

25. Violets. Woodcut from the *Grete Herbal*, London, 1525. About actual size.

illustrations, but shall content myself with remarking that in their almost comic way these pictures raise some of the most desperately serious problems that are known to man, for these problems are those of thought itself rather than of the materials with which it deals. There is a Latin tag which asks who it is that takes care of the caretakers. According to our temperaments we may laugh at these pictures or be condescending or up stage about them, but if we look at them intelligently they contain matter for the most humble prayer.

As a relief from such solemn notions as these, I may call

attention to one of the most amusing instances of trying to transform a verbal and therefore ideologically analytical and symbolic statement about shapes into a concrete visual image. In the *Hortus Sanitatis* of 1491 there is a description of the barnacle, which, as I remember, is said to be a fish that eats ships and has its bottom on top—which of course is a perfectly correct statement about the

26. Violets. Woodcut from Brunfels's *Herbarum vivae eicones*, Strassburg, 1530. Reduced.

shape of the creature that fastens itself under the hulls of ships. This statement much impressed the poor illustrator, who, accordingly, depicted a fish of some kind, with head, tail, fins and all the rest, but with claws, and, on its back, a very human bottom.

The first return to nature after the herbal of 1485 came when Brunfels issued, at Augsburg in 1530, the first volume of his celebrated herbal. This was illustrated with sharply observed and sensitively drawn woodcuts by Hans Weiditz. Weiditz is mentioned only in some laudatory verses in the first edition of the first volume. His remarkable woodcuts have been adversely criticized as being portraits of particular plants, showing not only their personal forms and characters but the very accidents of their growth, such as wilted leaves and broken stems, rather than being schematic statements of the distinguishing characteristics of the species and genera. In view of the fact that there was as yet nothing that could be called a workable classificatory system in botany, this criticism has always seemed to me to be a bit forehanded.

Twelve years later, in 1542, at Basel, Fuchs published his celebrated herbal, in which the abundant woodcut illustrations no longer represented particular plants but were careful schematic representations of what were considered the generic forms. They contain no indication of either the personalities or the accidents of growth of the plants. The illustrations were drawn from the actual plants by an artist named Albert Mayer, whose drawings were then copied on the blocks, and doubtless given their schematic form, by Heinrich Fullmaurer, after which the woodcutter, Hans Rudolph Speckle, did his work of cutting the blocks. We know this because at the end of the volume there are portraits of the three men at work, with their names and callings. These portraits are the first explicit statement I recall that a set of illustrations, although based on drawings specifically made for the purpose of illustrating a text, were, as actually printed, second-hand and not first-hand reports. This is the first time that both artist and woodcutter are given full recognition in the informational book they concerted to illustrate, and it is the first specific statement of the fact that the drawing on the block was not made by the original draughtsman but was a revised version of his drawing made by a specialist whose business it was to draw with lines that were suitable for their technical purpose. I shall have much to say about the inevitable results of this practice and its effects upon the communication of information and ideas. It is important to notice that in this first forthright example the result was no longer a portrait of a particular thing but a schematic representation of its generalized or theoretical generic forms. It thus represents not only one of the most important steps ever consciously taken in the

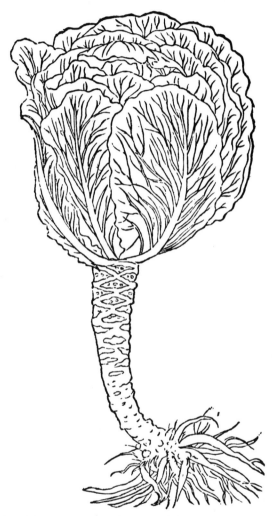

**Brafsicæ quartum genus.**
**Rappißkraut.**

27. 'Kappiskraut', woodcut from Fuchs's *De Stirpium Historia*,
Basel, 1545. Enlarged.

long search for a scientific classification of natural forms, but it also represents, quite unconsciously, one of the great steps in the substitution of rationalized statements of natural forms in place of the older, sometimes very good and sometimes very bad, attempts to represent the personal idiosyncrasies of such forms. In other words, it was a deliberate step away from the particular to the generalized, and as such is of the greatest importance in view of the subsequent history of visual information and the thought based on it.

Before leaving the fifteenth- and sixteenth-century woodcuts, it should be said that with few exceptions they were what are called 'facsimile' cuts, that is to say that the woodcutter's task was primarily to cut out the whites from between the lines of the artists' drawings on the blocks. This was, therefore, in theory not a translation or rendering but a preserving of the artist's drawing on the block. Some of the German woodcutters reached a very high degree of skill in their ability to cut out the whites without too much hurting the qualities of the lines. As examples I may mention the blocks for Holbein's *Dance of Death*, and for such prints by Dürer as his little round Virgin and Child after the engraving by Mantegna. There is strong reason to think that Dürer himself cut some of his earlier blocks, though many of the later ones were cut by professionals, some of whom are known to us by name.

Of the relief metal cuts of the late fifteenth century there is little to be said beyond the facts that comparatively few of them were made and that among them are the first examples of relief work in white on black grounds. Some of the white lines and dots were made by striking punches into the soft metal of the printing surfaces, much in the manner still used by silversmiths. Others were simply excavated with the ordinary engraving tool. The technical notion implicit in this latter method did not come into its own until the end of the eighteenth century in England, when for the first time it became common knowledge that an engraving tool could be used on a wooden block, provided the printing surface of the block was at right angles to its grain. As developed, this method of working on wood provided most of the nineteenth century's book and magazine illustration.

In the course of the first half of the sixteenth century what I may call the informational pressure on the woodcut illustration, that is, the cramming of more and more lines and detailed information into the given areas, became notable. This resulted in immediate difficulty for the printers, and probably explains why it was that such very finely detailed blocks as those for Holbein's *Dance of Death*, although presumably made about 1520, did not appear in book form until 1538. Wood-blocks, until the early years of the nineteenth century, were inked, as was type, not with rollers, as in our modern techniques, but by pounding them with large stuffed leather balls charged with ink. The least carelessness in the use of the balls produced spotty and clogged impressions, and this meant that good impressions could only be produced by very slow and correspondingly expensive press work. In the book form of the *Dance of Death*, two good impressions are followed by two poor ones, the good ones on the face of the paper and the poor ones on its back. This unevenness of impression could not be avoided by the printer of books with very fine cuts, because it came from the paper, which as made in those days was much smoother on one side than on the other. When the lines and the furrows in the paper were coarser than the lines on the block the tops of the lines in the paper took more ink from the block than did the furrows between them. There are many fine textured woodcut book illustrations of the middle of the sixteenth century which were rendered almost illegible by the streakiness that came from this.

By the fifteen-fifties the woodcut had reached the limit of minuteness of work beyond which it could not go so long as there was no change in the techniques of paper-making and of inking the blocks. Although a few fifteenth-century books had been illustrated with engravings, it was not until about the middle of the sixteenth century that there began, slowly and sporadically at

28. Otto Heinrich, Count Schwarzenburg. Portion of a woodcut by Tobias Stimmer (1539–1582). Enlarged.

29. Portion of an engraving by C. Cort (c. 1530–1571) after Titian. Enlarged.

30. Torso from an engraving of Bacchus by Goltzius (1558–1616). Enlarged.

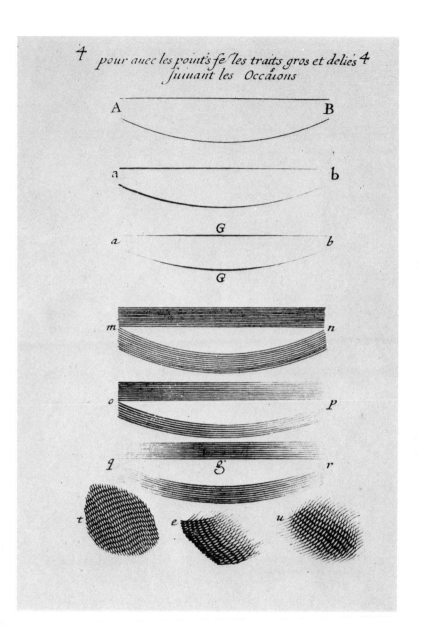

4 *pour auec les points se les traits gros et deliés* 4
*suiuant les Occâions*

31. A Page from Bosse's *Treatise on Engraving* of 1645.
Enlarged.

32. Portion of an early impression of Mantegna's engraving of the Bacchanal with the Wine Press. Enlarged.

33. The same portion of a late impression of the same engraving.

34. Head from the etched portrait of Frans Snyders by Van Dyck (1599–1641). Enlarged.

35. Head from the engraved portrait of Van Baelen by du Pont (1603–1658)
after Van Dyck. Enlarged.

36. Head from an engraving by Vorstermans (1595–1667) after a drawing of an ancient marble by Rubens. Reduced.

first and then with increasing commonness and regularity, the flood of books illustrated with engravings and etchings—processes which did not suffer from the limitations interposed by the paper and the method of inking.

An adequate explanation of these limitations would require a long and boring description of minute details, but it may be said that in spite of all our modern skills it is still a mechanically simpler task to ink and pull good clean impressions from microscopically fine lines sunk below the surface of a sheet of polished metal than it is to ink and pull good clean impressions from what in comparison are very coarse lines which stand up from a surface, whether it be of metal or wood. It depends on the difference between filling sunk lines with ink and then wiping away the excess of ink from the surface, and covering the tops of raised lines with ink and not being able to get rid of any excess of ink on the shoulders and sides of the lines. It also depends on the difference between squeezing softened paper into the ink contained in sunk lines and squeezing ink on the tops of raised lines into paper. We must always remember that while an etched or engraved line stands up above the surface of the paper, a woodcut or other relief line is sunk into the surface of the paper. The extent to which any line stands up from or lies below the surrounding paper has much to do with what is called quality of impression.

The engraved and etched copper plates were more expensive to make and use than wood-blocks. They were slower to print from and could not be made to yield such enormous numbers of impressions, but they were able to provide far more detail without getting so fine in texture that they wore out before a sizable edition could be run off from them. We shall see how in the late sixteenth and early seventeenth centuries the engravers worked out techniques of engraving that greatly increased the number of good impressions they could get from their plates.

For a while the woodcutters tried to compete with the copper engravers by imitating as best they could their linear techniques, as can be seen for example in the blocks made for the mid-century

49

Venetian publishers and in those by such northern artists as Amman and Stimmer, but the result was merely a generation of bad and streaked and spotty illustrations.

By early in the 1600's the pictorial woodcut had been driven from the pages of all but the smallest number of serious and elegant books. It lingered on in the chap-books and fly sheets made for sale to the peasants and the less educated classes, but retained its place in the purely decorative initials and head and tail pieces which were recognized as necessary parts of the printer's equipment. A few artistic single-sheet woodcuts were made during the seventeenth century, but their number is small and they were apt to be large and decorative rather than small and informative. Naturally, a few original prints managed to find their way into books, but they were unusual, and, in general, not having the fashionable textures that came from the interposition of the reproductive engraver between the artist and the printing surface, they were not popular.

The reign of the woodcut was over. The importance of this comes from the fact that with the woodcut's disappearance from the pages of books the original print, that is, the first-hand pictorial statement of facts, also almost vanished from the pages of books. This was a great but ignored event in the history of European eyesight and had consequences of the greatest importance.

# III

## SYMBOLISM AND SYNTAX

## A RULE OF THE ROAD

## THE SIXTEENTH CENTURY

M Y story has now reached a point at which it is necessary to give thought to some problems of a very
general nature. Awareness of them is essential to
an understanding of my argument. Many people
regard these problems as highly theoretical and of no practical
interest, but as I look back at my thirty years in an art museum it
seems to me that a great deal of my time was devoted to wrestling
with them as immediate and concrete difficulties. Here it is only
possible to call attention to them, for their careful analysis would
require a long and difficult treatise.

In the museum I learned the bitter way how inadequate words
are as tools for description, definition, and classification of objects
each of which is unique. I found that while I was not much interested in the actual processes which go on inside a man's brain and
nervous system, I was desperately interested in the extent to which
he could communicate the results of those processes. I also learned

that baptism is neither explanation, nor description, nor definition. Baptism, the giving of a name, is merely the tieing together in association of a particular object or quality and a particular word. For those who know both the names and the objects or qualities to which they belong, the names do away with any necessity for description, definition, and classification as means of identification. In many instances the more absurd the names are the better they are for their purposes. Thus, in the Metropolitan Museum at one time there was much sculpture that had to be rather elaborately identified when we wanted to talk about it at the lunch table, but there were two much-discussed pieces of sculpture, one Chinese, the other Greek, which somehow took names unto themselves. The Chinese statue was Charlie Murphy and the Greek one was Pink Billy. While these names were silly and irreverent, they were absolutely precise as identifications and they saved much time. Once a name of this kind becomes familiar it serves as an identification long after its original has vanished from earth or even if it has never existed, as for instance such names as Julius Caesar and Excalibur.

However, very few of the specific shapes, colours, and textures of objects have proper names, and in a way it is very lucky for us that they do not, because an even smaller number of persons have memories so excellent that they could use them. Much of what we disdainfully call trade and professional jargon is nothing other than names that we don't happen to know. Thus for many purposes the fact that most of our words are mere class designations gives them their greatest usefulness. But, also, a mere class designation may cover an infinitely large number of distinguishable things, or qualities, or actions. When we try to describe a particular object in such a way as to communicate an idea of its personality or unique character to someone who is not actually acquainted with it, all that we can do is to pile up a selected group of these class names, like rings about a peg, in such a way that they overlap but do not coincide. By doing this it is sometimes possible to communicate such information that the hearer may be able to identify the object when he sees it. But beyond that it is impossible for us to go with words, for the ipseity, the particularity of the object, its this-and-no-other-ness, cannot be communicated by the use of class names. If they could they would not be the things we think they are. Actual first hand acquaintance is the only thing that does the trick.

The only way that anyone can gain acquaintance with objects, as distinguished from knowledge of them, is through immediate sense awareness of them. It is thus necessary to keep clear the distinction between sensuous acquaintance on the one hand and knowledge by description on the other, for otherwise we are certain to fool ourselves on crucial occasions. We have many different ways of symbolizing both acquaintance and knowledge, but of them all the most important are words and visual images. Both words and visual images may very well be compared to fish nets. When a fisherman tell us that there are no fish in the bay to-day, what he really means is that he has been unable to catch any in his net—which is quite a different thing. The fish that are too big do not get into his net, and those that are too small simply swim through it and get away. So far as the fisherman is concerned fish are only such creatures as he can catch in his net. In the same way words and visual images catch only the things or qualities they are adequately meshed for. Among the things no word net can ever catch is the personality of objects which we know by acquaintance.

The only set of sense awarenesses for which we have succeeded in making nets that catch the personality of objects are those of vision, and even they catch only a certain portion of it. This method of symbolization is the making of pictures or images, which, unlike spoken words, are apprehended through the same sense organs which give us the awarenesses we try to symbolize. Practically speaking, the visual image is the only symbol we have that does not necessarily require the translation of a sensuous awareness into terms of some other associated sense awareness or else of some extremely limited, arbitrary, and artificial convention of correspondences. It is in these translations that we come to many of our misunderstandings. The translation of a sensuous awareness that comes to us through one set of nerve channels into that which comes to us through another set of nerve channels is accomplished by association. Thus, although it is literally impossible to see a noise, we have no hesitation in saying that we have seen a man making a certain sort of noise, although in fact we have not heard the noise and have only seen him going through motions that we associate with that noise. In this instance the phrase 'making a certain sort of noise' is merely an associational symbol for the complicated series of motions we actually saw the man make. So-called illusions can almost invariably be shown to have arisen, not because the sense awareness actually involved has given us a false report, but because we have dragged into our account of what happened associated awarenesses that come to us through other channels.

Thus the more closely we can confine our data for reasoning about things to data that come to us through one and the same sense channel the more apt we are to be correct in our reasoning, even though it be much more restricted in its scope. One of the most interesting things in our modern scientific practice has been the invention and perfection of methods by which the scientists can acquire much of their basic data through one and the same sensuous channel of awareness. I understand that in physics, for example, the scientists are happiest when they can get their data with the aid of some dial or other device which can be read by vision. Thus heat, weight, lengths, and many other things that in ordinary life are apprehended through senses other than vision have become for science matters of visual awareness of the positions of mechanical pointers.

In view of this it is worth while to examine a little more closely the differences between word symbols and visual symbols. Spoken words are addressed to the ear. Visual symbols are addressed to the eye. A printed or written word or sequence of them is addressed to the eye, but is immediately, as the result of long training and habit, translated into sounds addressed to the ear. Actually a sentence in print is composed of a number of superimposed symbols, each of which has only a vague and arbitrarily determined meaning. First, there are the letters of the alphabet, each of which is a conventional sign directing the man who sees it to make a series of muscular actions which, when fully executed, result in the making of a sound. Taken by themselves they have no meaning other than this conventionally assigned set of muscular actions. The letters of the Arabic or Hebrew alphabets have no meanings of this kind for those of us who are not acquainted with those languages. Many letter designs are made according to topological recipes. Thus the recipe for each Roman capital letter is simple, abstract, and completely arbitrary. Starting with the idea of a line and the distinctions between up and down and right and left, it is devoid of any requirement of particular shape, size, or proportion. The recipe for each letter can be analysed into the number of times a given number of lines intersect one another and the order in which the intersections occur. This permits of an infinite number of particular shapes for each letter. Thus, when we see a series of Roman capital letters we are called upon to recognize not any particular shapes but a series of representative members of particular classes of topologically defined forms. We call any member of the 'A' class 'a', and any member of the 'B' class 'b', and so on. The consequence of this is that when an instructor dictates a sentence to his class each student can write it down in his peculiar, personally adopted, set of letter shapes. Then, if all the copies are proof read and corrected, all the copies, in spite of their remarkable differences in particular shapes and general appearance, contain representative members of each letter class used in the sentence, arranged in the same linear order. Thanks to this all the sentences as written are identical in their verbal content.

Each written or printed word is a series of conventional instructions for the making in a specified linear order of muscular movements which when fully carried out result in a succession of sounds. These sounds, like the forms of the letters, are made according to arbitrary recipes or directions, which indicate by

55

convention certain loosely defined classes of muscular movements but not any specifically specified ones. Thus any printed set of words can actually be pronounced in an infinitely large number of ways, of which, if we leave aside purely personal peculiarities, Cockney, Lower East Side, North Shore, and Georgia, may serve as typical specimens. The result is that each sound we hear when we listen to anyone speaking is merely a representative member of a large class of sounds which we have agreed to accept as symbolically identical in spite of the actual differences between them. These differences are sometimes so marked that persons coming from different parts of the English speaking world can no more understand each other than if they were speaking completely different languages.

The meanings of the combinations of sounds we call words are also the result of convention or of special agreement, and none of them, unless it be a proper name, has any very precise or exact meaning. They all have meanings that we can look up in the dictionary, but these dictionary meanings are frequently many in number and quite different from one another. Also, and most importantly, these dictionary meanings are words themselves, and in their turn have only conventional meanings. We all know the difference in practice between using a dictionary that contains no illustrations and using one that contains a good many.

Actually, the meanings of many of the most used words depend on their contexts. More than that, their meanings also depend very largely on their syntactical use. To show this it is sufficient to take three words, such for example as 'James' and 'Henry' and 'kicked', and arrange them in sentences. Unless the context tells us we have no way of knowing whether one or each of the proper names represents a boy, or a man, or a mule. The meanings of the sentences made of these three words depend, in English at least, on the time order in which they are used. 'James kicked Henry' has obviously not the same meaning as 'Henry kicked James', while 'Henry James kicked' has a meaning that is comically and in every way different from that of either of the two other sentences.

This means that, when the very simple three-word sentences I have just used are printed, each contains at least six or seven different layers of symbolic practice, each layer being composed of vague arbitrarily determined representatives of classes of shapes or sounds, none of which, so far as concerns communication, has any specific shape or sound or meaning.

The only wonder about the system is that men are able to get along with it as well as they do. It certainly is not nicely calculated to convey either precise meanings or any definite idea of the character, personality, or quality of anything. This is shown by the fact that while it is comparatively easy to write a recipe for the making of a class of objects, such, for example, as popovers, it is impossible to tell anyone what a particular popover either looks like or tastes like. Because of this a great many of our so-called descriptions or definitions are no more than generalized instructions for the making of things, in other words, mere cook book recipes. This is also the reason that many so-called descriptions are merely accounts of very subjective feelings or emotions that an object has given rise to in the beholder. As fine examples of this I may refer to Mr. Ruskin's description of the façade of St. Marks and to Mr. Pater's description of the Mona Lisa.

As matter of fact, the moment that anyone seriously tries to describe an object carefully and accurately in words, his attempt takes the form of an interminably long and prolix rigmarole that few persons have either the patience or the intelligence to understand. A serious attempt to describe even the most simple piece of machinery, such, let us say, as a kitchen can-opener with several moving parts, results in a morass of words that only a highly trained patent lawyer can cope with, and yet the shape of that can-opener is simplicity itself as compared with the shape of such a thing as a human hand or face.

As we think about this it becomes obvious why the tool-maker wants not a written description of the device which he is called upon to make but a series of carefully made drawings accompanied by terse specifications of materials, dimensions, and, especially, of tolerances. A purely verbal description demands of the tool-maker that he take a series of arbitrary, abstract, vague, word symbols arranged in a linear order and translate them into concrete forms of material in a three-dimensional space in which there is no linear or time order and in which everything exists simultaneously. Someone may wonder at my phrase 'materials, dimensions, and, especially, tolerances', and ask what tolerances have to do with the problem. The tolerances are the so-called accuracies within which the so-called measurements have to be made. They are literally the tool-maker's recognition that so far as he is concerned there is no such thing as a precise measurement, that for him there is no such thing as 'three inches', but only 'three inches by and large'. Actually the tool-maker requires two tolerances for each dimension—one for the dimension itself, and one for the place from which the measurement of the dimension is to be taken. It simply goes to show that in the most exacting business of making instruments of precision there are no such things as exact and precise dimensions.

Furthermore, if you want to hold a tool-maker to a complete series of dimensions and tolerances for the several parts of an instrument of precision you must not also try to hold him to a series of overall dimensions and tolerances. In both logic and actual practice he can do one thing or the other, but not both. This is the reason for the rule, in shops where they make drawings for instruments of precision, never to indulge in 'double dimensioning', i.e. never to give both a complete series of dimensions and their sum. Always there must be some dimension or dimensions that are left to the discretion of the maker. It is merely a humble work-a-day solution of the ambiguity which the astrophysicist refers to as the non-integrability of displacement.

In its way the situation is analogous to the problem of classification of natural forms which is faced by botanists and zoologists. You divide your total number of forms into two classes—one a defined class you call A, the other an undefined class you call Not-A. You then divide the Not-A class into two sub-classes, one

of which you define and call B, and the other of which you do not
define and call Not-B. You proceed from there in the same
manner, by dividing the undefined classes into defined and undefined classes. Thus there is always an undefined remainder. So
soon as you try to break down a group of forms into classes in
such a way that you leave none of them undefined, you are certain
to be in trouble and to produce an impractical and unworkable
scheme—just because you are dealing with actual objects and not
with purely logical concepts. The actual object always has something about it that defies neat classification, unless you can manage
always to stay in the middle of your definition and not get out
towards its shadowy and slippery edges. In other words, our verbal
definitions are only good so long as we do not have to think just
what they mean. When we do have to think just what they mean
we are more than apt to wind up with a very temperamental and
wholly chance five to four decision.

Visual images, unlike verbal descriptions, address themselves
immediately to the same sense organs through which we gather
our visual information about the objects they symbolize. At one
end of their gamut they are completely abstract diagrams, such as
that of the drawing for the instrument maker about which we have
just been talking. There is an infinite number of ways of making
any such drawing and in the end they all come to the same thing—
for very much the same reason that sentences written from dicta-
tion by a number of persons, once they have been proof read and
conformed, all have the same symbolic meanings, despite their
marked differences in particular shapes and general forms. As a
matter of fact, practically all drawings of that kind are actually
proof read, but the man who does it is called a 'checker'. The only
reason he can do his work is that the lines in the drawing are mere
representatives of classes of lines and from that point of view can
hardly be called lines at all. Certainly they do not function as
particular lines. At the other end of the pictorial gamut we find
things like the micro-photographs which enable us to tell exactly
from which pistol a particular bullet was fired. In this latter case

the micro-photograph goes behind the general class description or definition and reaches the personality, the what for us is the 'this-and-no-otherness', of a machine which until that moment had been merely an unidentified member of a class without personality or individual character. This last class of visual statements not only cannot be proof read but, short of faking, cannot be conformed to what the proof reader calls 'copy'—and for the reason that there is no symbolic copy to read back to, but merely a concrete particular object. Should one of them be inaccurate or indistinct it has to be discarded, for it cannot be corrected. The probative value of a retouched photograph is singularly slight.

Visual statements are normally somewhere between the two ends of the gamut that have just been described. Some of them are purely schematic, and some of them are intended to catch the indicia of personality. An illustration in a botany or an anatomy can be almost purely schematic, for the thing it is intended to symbolize is not any particular instance of the shape of a concrete leaf or muscle, but a broad general class of shapes. However, when it comes to such things as the illustrations in a history of painting or sculpture what is desired is a visual statement of the characteristics or qualities which differentiate each work of art from every other work of art. These are not generalities but the most concrete and precise of particularities.

Before the days of photography and photographic process, it was impossible to hope for any such visual statement as that made by a photograph, and the most that could be asked for was a first-hand statement by a competent and honest observer and recorder.

The competent and honest observer and recorder, however, had his very distinct limitations. In the first place, he could only draw a selected and very small part of the things he did observe. More than that, courageous and sharp-sighted as he might be, he had learned to see in a particular way and to lay his lines in accordance with the requirements of some particular convention or system of linear structure, and anything that that way of seeing and that convention of drawing were not calculated to catch and

bring out failed to be brought out in his statement. For shortness'
sake I shall frequently refer to such conventions as syntaxes. Thus
the Germans of the Renaissance had one kind of vision and drawing and the Italians had another. Furthermore, when it came to
copying a picture, that is to making a visual statement about a
visual statement, the copyist felt under no obligation to be faithful
to either the particular forms or the linear syntax of the earlier
draughtsman he thought he was copying. Painstakingly and carefully as Dürer might copy a real rabbit or a violet in his own
syntax, when it came to copying a print by Mantegna he refused
to follow Mantegna's syntax, and retold the story, as he thought,
in his own syntax. I doubt if it ever occurred to him that in changing the syntax he completely changed both the facts and the story.
The comparison of the two, the Mantegna and the Dürer, is very
illuminating about a great many things.

Another important difference between visual statements and
collocations of word symbols, is that while there are dictionary
meanings for each of the word symbols, and while there may be
dictionary definitions for the names of the things symbolized by
a complex of lines and spots, there are no dictionary definitions
for the individual lines and spots themselves. It is much as though
we had dictionary definitions for sentences and paragraphs but
not for individual words. Thus while there is very definitely a
syntax in the putting together, the making, of visual images, once
they are put together there is no syntax for the reading of their
meaning. With rare exceptions, we see a picture first as a whole,
and only after having seen it as a whole do we analyse it into
its component parts. We can begin this analysis at any place in
the picture and proceed in any direction, and the final result is
the same in every case. It is a very different situation from that
exemplified in our little three-word sentences about Henry and
James, in which we have to begin with the component parts as
they are given to us in a time order and only after the sentence
is finished are able to effect a synthesis of them into a whole. This
leads me to wonder whether the constantly recurring philosophical

discussion as to which comes first, the parts or the whole, is not merely a derivative of the different syntactical situations exemplified on the one hand by visual statements and on the other by the necessary arrangement of word symbols in a time order. Thus it may be that the points and lines of geometry are not things at all but merely syntactical dodges.

I have a notion that much of the philosophical theory of the past can eventually be traced back to the fact that, whereas it was possible after a fashion to describe or define objects by the use of arbitrary and exactly repeatable word symbols addressed, mediately or immediately, to the ear, it was not possible to describe or define them by exactly repeatable images addressed to the eye. Of course, the ancients could make pictures of particular things, but their pictures were of little use as definitions or descriptions because they could not be exactly repeated, a thing that it is impossible to do so long as every copy of a picture has to be copied by hand. Pliny's account of the predicament of the Greek botanists is a striking example of how this worked out in practice. We have seen another very pretty example of it in the history of botanical illustration between the years 1480 and 1530.

A definition or description that cannot be exactly repeated is not only of little use but it introduces extraordinary complications and distortions. If it had been impossible ever to repeat exactly a verbal formula there would have been no law, no science, no religion, no philosophy, and only the most rudimentary animal technology—and it may be doubted that human beings would be able to communicate with each other much more effectively than so many geese or wild dogs.

Practically speaking, a definition or description that constantly undergoes changes does not help communication but interferes with it and results in a confusion greater than that which existed before it was attempted. It is to be remembered that the only statements the ancients knew which could be exactly repeated as often as was practically necessary were composed of word symbols which were mere representative members of classes. Under the

62

circumstances, I believe, it was only natural that the ancients came to think that there was some magic in words, of such a kind that they were real and that the shifting changing phantasmagorias of sensuous awarenesses they described were at best composed of imitations or faulty exemplifications of the reality that existed in the word. Plato's Ideas and Aristotle's forms, essences, and definitions, are specimens of this transference of reality fromt he object to the exactly repeatable and therefore seemingly permanent verbal formula. An essence, in fact, is not part of the object but part of its definition. Also, I believe, the well-known notions of substance and attributable qualities can be derived from this operational dependence upon exactly repeatable verbal descriptions and definitions—for the very linear order in which words have to be used results in a syntactical time order analysis of qualities that actually are simultaneous and so intermingled and interrelated that no quality can be removed from one of the bundles of qualities we call objects without changing both it and all the other qualities. After all, a quality is only a quality of a group of other qualities, and if you change anyone of the group they all necessarily change. Whatever the situation may be from the point of view of a verbalist analysis, from the point of view of visual awarenesses of the kind that have to be used in an art museum the object is a unity that cannot be broken down into separate qualities without becoming merely a collection of abstractions that have only conceptual existence and no actuality. In a funny way words and their necessary linear syntactical order forbid us to describe objects and compel us to use very poor and inadequate lists of theoretical ingredients in the manner exemplified more concretely by the ordinary cook book recipes.

Now, to come back to prints—the earliest engravers had no systematic system of shading or laying their lines. They covered any such portion of the plate as required to be shaded with a series of scratchy, scrabbly, lines, laid anyway. All that they asked of these lines was that they should give a tone to the spots where

63

they appeared. This can be seen, for example, in many of the so-called niello prints, in the 'fine manner' prints of the Florentine school, and in some of the more primitive prints of the German school. It may be that these prints represent the goldsmith's tradition of drawing. However, it was not long before trained draughtsmen began to make engravings, and as they did so they introduced into engraving their habitual methods of laying lines with their pens. Pollaiuolo and Mantegna drew firm carefully considered outlines, and shaded by using almost parallel lines running tilted from right to left without regard to the direction of the outlines. This gave somewhat the effect of flat washes of monochrome. In Germany the artists, true to their caligraphic habit of drawing, shaded with lines that had a tendency to follow the shapes, as can be seen in the prints of the Master E. S., Schongauer, and Dürer. The Italians spent most of their time and thought on their outlines, and their shading was primarily a rapid way of producing an added sense of three dimensionality. The Germans put as much time on the mechanical neatness of their shading and its calligraphic slickness as they did on their outlines. They also tried to combine with this all sorts of information about the local details and textures of the surfaces of the objects they represented. Like the Nature of the old physics books, the Germans hated what they thought of as a pictorial vacuum, and believed that a good honest workman should fill his plate from corner to corner. If I may put the matter in philosophical jargon, even the greatest of them saw objects located in a space that was independent of them and unrelated to their forms, whereas the greater Italians saw that space was merely the relation between objects. If you see in this latter way, the spaces between objects become just as important as the objects themselves, for they are actually part of the objects, even possibly their most important part. But the Germans never discovered this, and kept right on filling their plates with objects deprived of space. One result of this was that while the Italians not infrequently achieved a sense of volumes through the quality of their merest, baldest outlines, the

*Si non amplexus gustaßet Sanson amoris*
*Dalila non vires abripuißet ei.*

C. Mellan G. pinx. et f.                    Romæ Sup. pm.

37. 'Samson and Dalilah', an engraving by Mellan (1598-1688). Reduced.

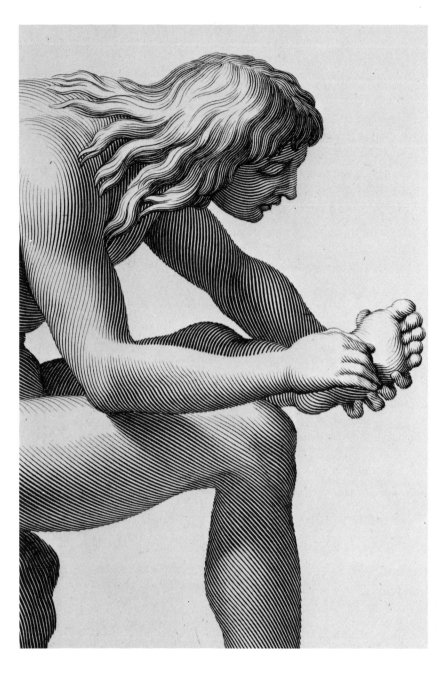

38. Portion of an engraving of 'The Spinello' by Baudet (c. 1636-1678).

39. Face from the engraved portrait of Pomponne de Bellelievre by Nanteuil
(1623–1678). Enlarged.

40. Modern half-tone of detail from the painting of 'Le Mezetin' by Watteau (1684–1721). Reduced.

41. The same detail from the engraving by Audran (1667–1756). About actual size.

42. Face from the engraving after 'L'Homme a l'œuillet' by Gaillard (1834–1887). Enlarged.

43. Head from an engraving by Caylus (1692-1765) after a chalk sketch by Watteau.
About actual size.

44. Figures from an etching of 'The Agony in the Garden' by Rembrandt 1606-1669). Enlarged.

Germans rarely or never achieved any sense of space or three dimensionality, much as they piled up contour within contour in their system of laying lines. Dürer, as I have shown elsewhere, actually worked out a system of perspective that resulted in a systematic denial of the homogeneity of space. Much of the peculiar psychological quality of his work can be traced directly to this. His various figures and architectural settings frequently have nothing to do with one another and exist in different spaces.

Incidentally, the Germans began to superimpose neat tidy systems of lines running in different directions and thereby produced a shimmer or play of textures that gave a sparkle to their prints, much as though they were textiles woven with several kinds of threads running through each other in different directions. In a way it may be compared to the patterns of the damask table cloths of our youths. While this superposition of systems of lines was easy for the pen draughtsman and for the engraver, it was not practical on the wood-block, for there it infinitely complicated the task of the woodcutter called upon to dig out the whites from between the pen lines on his blocks. Because of this, for example, the linear web of Dürer's engravings is not the same as that to be found in his woodcuts.

Marc Antonio, originally a Bolognese engraver of the primitive goldsmith type, wandered to Venice shortly after 1500, and while there produced engraved copies or piracies of Dürer's woodcuts of the *Life of the Virgin*, which are famous in the literature of prints for various reasons of no material interest. He also made copies of a few of Dürer's engravings. Out of this experience were eventually to come several things of great importance. Without discussing Marc Antonio's artistic abilities, it suffices to say that he spent much of his later life in Rome producing engraved versions of designs by such artists as Raphael and Peruzzi, as well as of ancient sculpture. The details of his relationship with Raphael are vague, indefinite, and unreliable. The earlier copyist engravers who had worked after Mantegna's pen drawings had simply copied the lines that Mantegna made with his pen. But Raphael's drawings were not of that type. His outlines were broken, and within these there was no close system of shading, but they conveyed an amazing sense of three-dimensionality, that is of volumes. Dürer and his German predecessors were practically devoid of this sense for volumes. Some way had to be devised of conveying this so important sense for volumes in the engravings after Raphael's drawings. Here Marc Antonio's experience in copying Dürer gave him the answer, but one that was far different from anything that Dürer himself ever did. Taking elements from Dürer's two different linear systems, that for his woodcuts and that for his engravings, Marc Antonio devised a kind of shading that represented not the play of light across a surface, and not the series of local textures, but the bosses and hollows made in a surface by what is under it. In a way it corresponds closely enough to the kind of drawing that is familiar in the maps of the geodetic surveys. With the curious Italian logic of his time he reduced this to a sort of rudimentary grammatical or syntactical system. Lucas of Leyden, fascinated by this, ceased to be an inspired teller of fairy tales and became a great theoretical grammarian of the engraved line. The followers of the two men in the south and the north eventually developed the idea into a very full fledged linear syntax. The phrase that Professor Saintsbury used in describing what he called English Augustan prose style may be applied to it. It was a most adequate instrument for an average purpose. It was fitted for the average skill of the average engraver, for it enabled him to produce tidy organized linear webs that called for no mental alertness. It could be learned as a routine. Marc Antonio's invention of it undoubtedly had much to do with the great esteem in which his work was held during the long reign of reproductive line engraving.

While this syntactical development was taking place, print publishing came into being as a specialized, specific trade. Prior to this time, so far as the records seem to show, goldsmiths and painters had made engravings with their own hands, professional engravers had worked independently for their own profit, and some of them had copied or pirated the drawings and prints of

66

other men. The earliest corpus of etched work, that of the Hopfer family of Augsburg, consists almost entirely of rapidly made copies of other men's work. Etching was the quickest way there was of getting out prints. For many years this was undoubtedly its principal virtue in the eyes of the trade. But the print publisher, unlike the painters and the independent engravers, was a capitalist entrepreneur. He hired men to make prints for him, which he stocked, and published, and dealt in just as though he were an ordinary manufacturer-dealer. He owned the plates and they represented a large part of his invested capital. His only reason for being in the business was to make money.

Lafreri in Rome and Cock in Antwerp may be taken as typical of the tribe. They determined what their prints should look like, just as they determined what they should represent. Lafreri discovered the horde of travellers who came to Rome and wanted to take home with them pictures of what they had seen there. So he had prints made which he sold singly, or in sets, or in complete collections. Cock in the north, himself an engraver, also realized the popularity of Italian paintings and subjects, so he made drawings of them and had other artists make them for him, and then had the drawings engraved in his shop by his employees. He did the same thing for the work of the popular northern painters. Pieter Brueghel the elder provided him with many drawings of landscapes and satirical subjects to be engraved.

In the course of this commercial development a curious thing happened. Functions that had been filled by one man got split apart in a specialization of labour. The painter painted. The draughtsman for the engraver copied in black and white what the painter had painted, or the Roman view, or ancient statue. The engraver rendered the drawings of these draughtsmen. The engravings in consequence were not only copies of copies but translations of translations. Except where the engraver had before him a pen-drawing, such as one of Brueghel's, which was at one and the same time an original work of art and a detailed set of plans and specifications for the lines of the engraving which the engraver could copy as directly and slavishly as some of the early copyists had copied the drawings of Mantegna, he—the engraver, that is—had to translate all the various kinds of drawings that came to him into some kind of standardized linear system. That is what happens in shop work done for an entrepreneur whose name is signed to the finished work. The 'house' develops a style and a quality by which it is known and which it does not willingly part from after it has become known. It is part of its 'good will'. This is one of the reasons that etchers and engravers who have been tied to particular publishers are so apt to show little artistic development in their work and to make so few experimental plates. What their employer wants from them is just what the farmer wants from his laying hens, a regular production of eggs of the same standardized size, colour, and weight. The only way to secure this is through the adoption of a syntax of the laying of lines for an average purpose. What Marc Antonio and Lucas of Leyden had adventuresomely started was reduced to a wholesale practice and technique of the standardized article.

Of course this development was not as simple and direct as my account of it, for there have always been artists who have thought and worked in their own ways, making works of art. However, in the vast field of prints for information, for profit, for propaganda, for sale to anyone and everyone, I believe my account is substantially true. It is important to observe that this development took place just in the period when the shift from the woodcut to the copper plate began in the illustration of books—and my account is borne out by the illustrated books and the countless sets of views and allegories and beauties and fancy subjects and pieties that lumber up the great European collections and the dusty shops on such streets as the Rue Bonaparte and the Rue des Beaux Arts. The names of the most proficient practitioners appear lumped together in the dreariest paragraphs of the conscientious historians. What we forget, however, in our boredom with these dull things, is that it was exactly they which constituted the back bone of the print trade and which gave the world such visual information as it had of the things represented in them. The great influence of Italy on the north, and later that of Paris on the rest of Europe, was exerted through reproductive prints which carried the news of the new styles. If we would understand those influences and the forms they took, we must look not at the Italian and Parisian originals but at what for us are the stupid prints which the publishers produced and sold in such vast quantities. This is a point that is all too often overlooked by art historians.

Standing out from the dull industrious day labourers in the vineyard there was a little group of virtuosi of the engraver's tool, whose names and performances were famous so long as the world had to depend on engravings for its information about the shapes of things that were not at hand for inspection. As always happens when there is a distinction between the creative artist and the performer, as for example in music and on the stage, people lose their sense of discrimination. The performer ceases to be a puppet moved by the creator and becomes a person in his own right. People knew Garrick's *Hamlet* and not Shakespeare's. The self-assertiveness of the performer shows itself in the invention of mannerisms and tricks calculated to call attention to himself at the cost of the explication of the creator's ideas. Where the creator creates characters and situations, the performer exhibits and emphasizes himself, and, curiously, he does this even when he writes the plays in which he is the star actor. A very great deal of the standard history of prints is devoted to prints, both 'original' and 'reproductive', which are neither more nor less than the performer's assertions of his own physical personality. Thus in engraving there were performers who made great specialties of the rendering of glass and shiny metal, of silks and furs, and of foliage and whiskers. It is impossible to think that even so great an artist as Dürer was not tainted by this sort of virtuosity. The virtuoso engravers chose the pictures they were to make or reproduce not for their merits but as vehicles for the exhibition of their particular skills. The laying of lines, swelling and diminishing, the creation of webs of crossed lines, of lozenges with little flicks and dots in their middles, the making of prints in lines that all ran parallel or around and around—one engraver made a great reputation by the way he rendered the fur of a pussy cat, and another made a famous head of Christ that contained but one line, which beginning at the point of the nose, ran around and around itself until it finally got lost in the outer margin,—stunts such as these became for these exhibitionists not a way of saying something of interest or importance but a method of posturing in public. Naturally the great showmen became the models of the less gifted but equally stupid routine performers, for all these trick performances contained far more of laborious method than of eyesight or draughtsmanship.

The webs spun by these busy spiders of the exactly repeatable pictorial statement were in some respects much like what the geometers call the 'net of rationality', a geometrical construction that catches all the so-called rational points and lines in space but completely misses the infinitely more numerous and interesting irrational points and lines in space. The effect of these rationalized webs on both vision and visual statement was a tyranny, that, before it was broken up, had subjected large parts of the world to the rule of a blinding and methodically blighting visual common sense. What was not according to the book of deportment for the makers of exactly repeatable pictorial statements was not only 'not done', but, worse, it was bad manners.

# IV

## THE TYRANNY OF THE RULE

## THE SEVENTEENTH AND
## EIGHTEENTH CENTURIES

I N the first half of the seventeenth century five very remarkable men made or published prints. Roughly speaking they were contemporaries. Between them they had great influence on the kinds of prints that were to be made for a long time. For three of them print-making was a business, a business to be minded just as carefully as any other commercial undertaking. These three were Rubens, Callot, and Bosse. Another made prints to please himself, apparently paid no attention to commercial considerations, and died in an asylum. This man was Hercules Seghers. The fifth man was Rembrandt, who went bankrupt years before he died and, never being discharged, had thenceforth little interest in money-making. Thanks to the later development of photography and photographic process, while we remember a good many prints of the Seghers-Rembrandt tradition, we have forgotten all but a very small part of the prints that came out of the Rubens-Callot-Bosse tradition, except as oddities that we sometimes see in old-fashioned houses and collections.

71

Sir Peter Paul Rubens, an ambassador, a knight, an internationally famous painter, and especially, a very astute and successful business man, saw the great financial advantage to be gained by having engravings made after his paintings and selling them in large editions. Some of the prints after his pictures are the work of outsiders working for their own accounts and purposes, but a great many of them were published either by Rubens himself or by firms in which he was a partner. There are said to be early trial proofs of some of these engravings which are worked over in pen and ink to indicate corrections and changes that were to be made in them, much as though they were author's galley proofs. The handwriting in these pen lines has been recognized as that of Rubens himself. The only touched proof of a Rubens print that I know of in America is in the Metropolitan Museum. It is a counterproof of the first state of an etching of St. Catherine, by Rubens himself. Perhaps it is the only print he made with his own hands.

What this means is that Rubens organized a school or group of engravers who worked under his immediate supervision and presumably in his pay. For their translations of his paintings and sketches into black and white they devised a linear scheme which answered two quite different requirements. Not only was it desirable to construct a linear network that should be the instrument of an average Rubensy purpose, but it was just as desirable to find a method of incising the copper in such a way that the plates would yield very large editions before they began to show appreciable wear.

Until photography and photographic process took the place of the reproductive print made by the older processes, the size of the edition that could be pulled from a plate was a matter to which almost all print-makers, original as well as reproductive, gave much thought. The great discovery that a larger profit could be made from the snobbery to which a limited edition appeals is comparatively recent, and can be regarded as one of the *sequelae* of the pervasion of photographic process. Seymour Haden was,

72

perhaps, the last of the well-known etchers who was old-fashioned enough to regard his plates as bonds from which he might at regular intervals take off the coupons he called proofs. To do this he adopted the trick, invented in Paris in his youth, of 'steel facing' his plates so that he might be able to keep on printing discreet editions of his etchings and dry points over periods that in some instances lasted for about forty years. Steel facing was not available to the print-makers of the seventeenth and eighteenth centuries, and so they had to give thought to the depth of their lines and their distances apart, for shallow lines and lines that were too close together wore out in the most disheartening way.

With these requirements as their basis the Rubens school of engravers worked out a linear net that was most admirable from the point of view of Rubens himself. It was actually one of the most successful instruments of an average purpose that has ever been devised. Any sketch, no matter how fleeting its indications, and any most elaborately detailed oil painting of the Rubens type, could be tossed into the hopper of the engraving shop, and out of the other end would come a print that had all the familiar trade-marked Rubens look. They all looked alike when they were finished. It was through these prints that Rubens's international influence was exercised. Two of the greatest events in the history of landscapes, whether painted, engraved, or etched, are the engravings after, first, Brueghel, and, second, Rubens.

Callot was a professional etcher, not a painter who also etched. The distinction is important. It is significant that so few of the original prints by men who were not primarily painters are remembered. Callot was greatly influenced by the fashion for swelling lines that had been started in the second half of the sixteenth century by the virtuoso engravers. One of the greatest of these virtuosi was Goltzius. As we shall see, this swelling and diminishing of schematically laid lines had its immediate economic aspects as well as those of mere fashion. The engravers after Rubens were naturally and easily influenced by the full-blown Goltzius type of linear work. Etching, however, was much quicker than engraving, but the ordinary etching needle did not lend itself to the creation of the swell and diminuendo of the individual lines as did the engraver's tool. To achieve this it was necessary for Callot to use a specially designed etching point that is called the *échope*. Whether he invented it I do not know, but he was the first to use it brilliantly and successfully. When used with care in the laying of lines that are systematically and not freely drawn, it enables its user to produce a very fair imitation of the swelling engraved line. It is often difficult to tell with the unaided eye whether a line in a print by Callot is an etched or an engraved line, especially because, as he used the old hard etching ground, it was possible for him to sink his engraving tool in an etched line before the ground was removed from the plate, and so give it its final polish and finish. His work was extremely popular, he printed large editions, and there were many copies and piracies of his prints, which very early became the object of assiduous attention from the collectors. The earliest literary account of the foibles of the typical print collector is to be found in La Bruyère's *Characters*, which was first published in 1688. The prints cited by La Bruyère are those of Callot. There is so much of method in Callot's work that the copyist-forger was frequently very successful in his imitations. This is one of the little penalties of methodical and schematic work, no matter how brilliant or direct it may appear.

Bosse was a small but active manufacturer of prints who took a great interest in theoretical matters. A friend and pupil of Desargues, he wrote important books on architecture, on stereotomy, and on perspective. He also wrote the first technical treatise on engraving and etching. He utilized Callot's tool for the production of etched lines that swelled and diminished, and that for their full effect had to be schematically laid. He also told how etching could be used for the preliminary work on a plate, after which it could be finished with the engraving tool. It was a technical trick that saved time and labour, and thus became very common among reproductive engravers. In the course of time, in one or another of its forms, it became a standard practice.

Bosse's book on etching and engraving of 1645 was not only the first on its subjects, but for more than a century it remained the standard one. It went through a number of editions, and a hundred and twenty years after its first publication it was edited and brought down to date by Cochin. A comparison of the first and last editions is very interesting and suggestive, for much had happened between them—especially the introduction of the modern soft etching ground in place of the old hard one.

Bosse's ideal was the tidy, regular, systematized, linear structure to which I have referred as a net of rationality. Some of the sentences in the introduction to his book are so interesting in view of the economics of print manufacture that I shall quote them. His prose style is as untidy as his prints were precise and regular, and so it is impossible to turn them literally into English and at the same time make sense of them. In my versions I have tried to play fair with both Bosse and my readers.

In the first place, Bosse clearly distinguishes between pictorial invention and composition on the one hand and linear quality and structure on the other hand. Little as he may have suspected it he was proceeding along the lines of the old Aristotelian-Scholastic distinction between substance and attributable qualities. It is a distinction that has only gone out of fashion in print-making and appreciation during the present century. Thus he says: 'The first among those to whom I have obligation is Simon Frisius, the Dutchman, who, in my opinion, should have great glory in this art, in as much as he handled the point with great mastery, and in his hatchings strongly imitated the neatness and firmness of the engraver's tool. . . . I speak only of the neatness of his etched lines, leaving aside the invention and the composition (*dessein*), it not being my intention to talk of such things.' He then says that 'Callot greatly perfected this art', and that 'if it had not been that his genius carried him to little figures, he would doubtless have done in big etchings all that can be done in imitation of the engraver's tool'. After this he makes a statement, which throws light not only on an aesthetic matter but very distinctly on an economic

75

one. 'For myself, I admit that the greatest difficulty I have met in etching is to make hatchings that swing, big, fat, and thin, as needed, as the engraver's tool does, and with which the plates may be printed for a long time.' It is interesting to notice, in view of this, that the present-day commonness of the various editions of his book implies that they were printed in large editions, and that the last edition, which was printed more than a hundred and twenty years after the first one, was still illustrated with impressions from many of the plates he made for the first edition. Bosse then makes an apology and defence of his attitude: 'It is not that I do not appreciate work done in etching that has not this neatness . . . but all will agree with me that it is the invention, the beautiful outlines, and the touches, of those who have worked the other way which makes their work appreciated rather than any neatness of the way they laid their lines. I believe that those who etched the other way would have acquired greater success in their business if they had availed themselves of my system of laying lines.' Here we have a clear-cut statement of the reasoning of the commercial print manufacturer. It would be hard to make a more practical definition of a tool for an average purpose, in which accuracy of representation of the personal characteristics of things was not as important as their reduction to an economically advantageous neatness of syntactical statement.

At the end of his book Bosse devotes several pages to printing —but with the remark that it is a different business. It is obvious from this that in his time printing was not regarded as a thing that the engraver or etcher should do himself. We have travelled a long way since that time. Then the test of a man's ability as a printer was how much alike he could get a long series of impressions. In Whistler's time it was seriously advanced that the etcher's artistry as printer was shown by how many different kinds of impressions he could pull from the same plate. That can be regarded as the erection of a technical incompetence into an artistic virtue.

In his discussion of the use of the engraver's tool Bosse gives one little detail that is of considerable interest—he tells how to remove the burr from the sides of engraved lines. He makes no comment upon this, but takes it for granted that it is to be done. The reason was twofold. It is not desirable that the impressions from a plate in which the lines have been schematically laid should be too rich, as that interferes with the brilliance which is one of the chief attractions of that kind of linear work. Also, and more important still, the deliberate removal of the burr in the beginning, instead of waiting for it to wear off in the course of printing the edition, meant that a very much larger number of impressions could be run off before there was any appreciable difference in quality among them. The early masters did not remove the burr from their plates, with the result that their early impressions are much richer than the somewhat later ones and have quite a different quality. This is very marked in the engravings by Mantegna and by Lucas of Leyden. When either had finished one of his plates it contained a good many very shallow lines with a good deal of burr. As soon as the burr vanished, his plates became pale and ghostlike. They are only to be understood in very early impressions of a kind that are extremely difficult to come by. Dürer, always keen about the economic aspects of his work, seems to have produced more evenly printed editions than his contemporaries, great as may be the difference between a very early impression from one of his plates and a somewhat later one. His rectification of an oversight in his engraving of the Prodigal Son is illuminating about his practice. He forgot to do part of a tree in the background and at the last minute, after the plate had had its burr diminished, he put it in, but forgot to work it down, with the result that the early impressions of this plate show a very strong burr on some of the lines of that tree. It would seem to indicate that he did not do his own printing. The impressions of the engravings by many of the early masters were at their most brilliant just when the burr had worn away and before there was any wear of the lines themselves. In the eighteenth and early nineteenth centuries, when people, accustomed to several centuries of brilliant schematic well scraped line work, had come to value their contemporary engravings for their brilliance and not for their richness or colour, it was these 'silvery' impressions of the older print-makers, printed just at the right moment in the wear of the plate, that were most sought for and highly valued. It is merely another instance of how a later period prizes things for qualities that are different from those that gave them their values when they were made, for the artists who made the old engravings judged them by how the lines looked before the plates showed wear.

The strong persistence of the ideal of the business-like systematized technique of draughtsmanship and of working the plate in such a manner that a large edition could be run off from it before it showed any material deterioration, is exhibited in Mr. Hind's opinion of 1908 that the greatest of the portrait etchers was not Rembrandt but Van Dyck. He says that Van Dyck produced plates 'which are perhaps the most perfect models of portrait etching in existence', and that Rembrandt cannot claim such praise, for although his work 'is even more wonderful in its penetrating genius than that of Van Dyck', 'it is essentially inimitable and has perhaps never succeeded except in the hands of the master himself. Van Dyck on the other hand has remained the pattern of the best of modern portrait etchers' (by which, as appears elsewhere in his book, Mr. Hind meant Legros and William Strang), and his portraits make 'a far more direct and intimate appeal' than those of Rembrandt. It is interesting to notice that in his *History of Engraving and Etching,* from which I have quoted with his kind permission, Mr. Hind did not mention that supreme example of portraiture on the copper, Rembrandt's 'Young Haaring', a print as far removed from the tradesman's ideals of longevity and easy brilliance as can be imagined.

Mr. Hind calls attention to the fact that when Van Dyck started his set of portrait etchings, which is known as his *Iconography,* it was a failure because the public demanded 'more finished work', and that the scheme was finally carried out by a long series of engravings of the Rubens school after sketches which Van Dyck supplied for the purpose. Of these perfunctory and stupid prints

78

Mr. Hind says that it was 'the elaborated engravings of the *Iconography* that formed the pre-eminent factor in fixing a standard for future engravers of portrait'. Mr. Hind was right, but the fact to which he calls attention is a very sorry and most important commentary upon many things.

Seghers, a little known artist, whose prints are of the greatest rarity, made many experimental plates, in which he indicated many of the ways that were to be travelled by etchers in the future. He not only sometimes printed his plates in coloured ink on coloured sheets of paper, but he made many landscapes that had a great influence on Rembrandt and a few of his contemporaries in the Dutch school. One of his plates was actually reworked by Rembrandt, who inserted large figures in a landscape, and others of them were probably the first original etchings of the low-lying Dutch countryside. Several of them were reworked and republished by Everdingen.

Rembrandt, the patron saint of non-commercial etchers, was a prolific etcher as well as a painter, but in both media he worked as differently from Rubens and Callot and Bosse as possible. The chronological sequence of his prints shows that in his development he strove to achieve expressiveness and neither systematization of his linear structure nor long life for his plates. Following Seghers in free experimentation, Rembrandt used etching, engraving, dry point, and what is called sulphur tint, on his plates. The sulphur tint was a way of producing extremely delicate tints that wore out with astonishing speed. The dry point burr also wore out very fast. Although many of his plates are in practically pure etching, he frequently used combinations of the media I have mentioned. It is doubtful whether any of his predecessors had been so 'impure' a worker. Dürer, on occasion, used a touch of dry point in his engraving, as in the 'Promenade', but was usually careful to cut away the burr before printing. He made only three pure dry points and five etchings. Lucas of Leyden, in 1520, mixed etching with engraving on the same plates, but seemingly did very few plates that way. I know of no print carried through in engraving by

79

Rembrandt, but he frequently used the engraver's tool to point up his etchings, and sometimes, as in the 'Diana Bathing' and the 'Dr. Bonus', used it for important passages while the rest of the plate was etched. A number of his later plates were carried through in practically pure dry point. He used touches of sulphur tint in some of his finest portraits. It is doubtful if any other print-maker of comparable rank ever made such drastic changes in the composition of his plates as Rembrandt did in his great dry points of the 'Large Three Crosses' and the 'Christ Presented to the People'. The only meaning of this can be that he did not care about the limitation which such practices put on the size of his editions. Moreover he had at no time a standardized scheme for the laying of his lines. His shading was done for light and shade and especially for colour, and not for surface bosses and hollows. All his drawing was highly autographic and idiosyncratic. At the end of his career as etcher, it can be said, he had no technique; that he knew only particular occasions and needs and invented ways of meeting them as they arose. For this reason during his own life he had little influence outside the small group around him. The men who exert what is called influence in a quasi-commercial occupation such as print-making are those who provide plainly stated and ready made recipes for the use of others.

In Rembrandt's own time and through the eighteenth century his greater masterpieces were not according to the doctrines of the dominant Rubens-Callot-Bosse tradition. It is interesting to observe how such an authority as Bartsch at the end of the eighteenth and the beginning of the nineteenth centuries was bothered by the greatest of Rembrandt's prints, just as he was by those of Mantegna, who, he said, had great genius but was a bad engraver. Rembrandt had to wait until the high tide of romanticism in the nineteenth century before his most remarkable accomplishments were recognized. Until past the middle of the nineteenth century all the world credited him with many etchings which obviously he could never have made. His influence, when it finally arrived, was among a group of etchers none of whom had his

45. Portion of a mezzotint by Lucas (1802-1881) after Constable. Enlarged.

46. Figure from the aquatint 'Por que fue sensible', from Goya's Caprichos
of 1803. Enlarged.

47. 'The Ecchoing Green', from Blakes' *Songs of Innocence* (1789). About actual size.

48. Portion of Daumier's relief print 'Empoignez les tous', from *Le Magasin Charivarique*, 1834. About actual size.

49. Three impressions of a wood-engraving from
Bewick's *Land Birds* (1797). (*a*) a proof on China
paper ; (*b*) from the textless edition of 1800 ; (*c*) from
the edition of 1832, on better paper. Enlarged.

50. Portion of Nesbit's wood-engraving of Rinaldo and Armida, 1822, on
China paper. Enlarged.

51. The same portion of the same engraving by Nesbit, on good book paper. Enlarged.

52. Two 'facsimile engravings' of drawings on
the block, from *Puckle's Club*, 1817, one on China
paper, the other on good book paper. About
actual size.

53. Two wood engravings from Thornton's *Eclogues of Vergil*, 1822. One by Blake, the other anonymous. About actual size.

54. Portion of Harvey's wood engraving of the 'Death of Lucius Quintus Dentatus'. Shortly before 1820. Enlarged.

55. The classical statue of Niobe and her Daughter, as engraved on wood from the *Penny Magazine* in 1833. Reduced.

56. Portion of a proof of a wood engraving of a drawing on the block by Daumier, for *Le Monde Illustré*, in the 1860's. Enlarged.

ability to draw or to compose, and none of whom had any imagination or human sympathies. The fact that he often thought out his technical procedure instead of following a mere recipe, was seized upon as justification for a great deal of technical incompetence that carried with it few compensating qualities. Actually, the so-called Revival of Etching that took place in the mid-nineteenth century was merely a revolt from the extreme technical capacity of the descendants of the Rubens-Callot-Bosse reproductive tradition in favour of a greater freedom of handling. But it was not a revival of the art and craft of etching, which so far from having disappeared had actually reached a state of amazing technical control over the laying of the lines, the biting, and the printing of the plate. Thus Rembrandt, who was the most highly disciplined and trained of workers, became the patron saint of a group of hasty sketchers who set up sketchiness as the criterion of what they liked to call 'the true function' of etching. It is to be doubted whether any other etcher, no matter of what school or time, has ever produced plates which required such careful technical forethought and planning as, for example, Rembrandt's 'Presentation in the Temple in the Dark Manner' or his portrait of the Young Haaring.

I shall comment upon the work of only a very few of the horde of later engravers who, in different countries, achieved reputation by following and developing the several variant recipes for standardization of linear work. A time sequence of the works of the French portrait engravers of the seventeenth century brings out with great clarity this search for system. At the beginning we find such an artist as Mellan using a system of shading by parallel lines with little and sometimes no cross-hatching. Later, Nanteuil, a great virtuoso of the engraver's tool, and a quite perfect representative of the intellectual attitude of the reign of Louis XIV, developed an elaborate system of flicks and cross lines, in which can be clearly seen the germs of that final degradation which, in the nineteenth century, took its name from the bank-note portraits from which all personality of both sitter and engraver had vanished. His need for system was closely related to the fact that much of the work on his plates was done by assistants. Nanteuil's discipline sat so hard upon him that there is no discernible difference between the portraits he did after his own drawings and those he made after portraits by other men. What came through into the print in either case was only what could be caught and held by his deliberately contrived net of rationality, which was invented for the purpose of portraying the masks that did duty for the faces of the men in high places under the King.

Audran, at the end of the century, had a direct influence on the system. He was perhaps the outstanding member of the group of engravers who reproduced the tapestries and other decorations of the palace at Versailles. The plates were so big and there were so many of them that speed was of the essence, and the liberal use of etching in them provided the only way of achieving it. There was little or no retouching or polishing up.

After Watteau's death in 1721, his wealthy friend Jean de Jullienne embarked upon a great plan to immortalize his memory by subventioning and publishing the two long series of engravings after his work that are known by the catch titles of the 'Big Watteau' and the 'Little Watteau'. The big one contained reproductions of Watteau's paintings, the little one reproductions of his drawings. They were originally issued as sets, the big one being limited to one hundred copies of 'first proofs'. No one had previously undertaken to present to the world at one time a corpus of prints representing as many as possible of the paintings and drawings of an artist. The character of Watteau's works was the antithesis of that of the great machines that decorated Versailles. It was desired to represent this character as closely as possible in the prints, and not to have it boiled down to the stiff consistency of a highly systematized and rigid linear texture. For this purpose Jullienne called to his aid the younger Audran and, especially, Tardieu and Boucher. They used etching and engraving, plain and mixed, to achieve their ends. It was a highly novel undertaking. Out of it there came a series of prints that are remarkable for their lightness, their blond sparkle, and their wit. It is doubtful if the general character of an artist's work had ever before been more boldly, more summarily, or more charmingly, translated into another medium. The technical means by which this was achieved is perhaps most easily to be observed in the plates reproducing the chalk and sanguine heads and figures which Watteau made as studies for his paintings. The media used in these studies were crumbly and not smooth and slick like the traditional pen and wash drawings which went to the ordinary engravers. More than that they were deft and light handed as few drawings that have ever been made. The way in which the feeling for these qualities was preserved or indicated in the prints after the drawings is one of the major triumphs of reproductive engraving, but, having been made without any apparent systematization or difficulty, it has rarely been recognized for what it actually is.

Shortly after the Jullienne publications were finished several technical innovations were made by the reproductive print-makers in their desire more closely to approach the character of original drawings. I have no doubt that the French fashion for framed drawings, which came in with the Regency style in interior decoration, had much to do with it. Aquatinting was developed to imitate wash drawings, roulettes were introduced with which to make crumbly lines like those of chalk, stipple was developed to make imitations of drawings lightly washed with colour, soft ground was invented to imitate the quality and texture of pencil drawings. Any and many of these processes were used on the same plates, and many prints were made in colour. The colour prints after the water-colours and gouaches of such an artist as Hubert Robert, in spite of all our modern improvements, still hold their charm and interest. Some of the small portraits in colour, such as one of Mme Bertin, are marvels of delicacy and brilliance. The engravers began to put forth what were called 'facsimiles' instead of translations.

While these things were happening there also grew up in France a fashion for very small and finely worked portraits, and, under the lead of such engravers as the younger Drevet and Ficquet, incredibly minute work was done, sometimes in pure engraving, sometimes in an indissoluble mixture of many techniques. In many of these prints the lines and dots are too small to be separately studied by the unaided human eye. One of the prices paid for this minuteness of scale was that the so finely reticulated surfaces wore out very fast.

At the end of the century someone invented the physionotrace —a contraption with which it was possible for an itinerant portraitist to make quick and easy tracings of profiles and transfer them to the copper in small size. Another device much used at this time was the camera obscura, quickly followed by the camera lucida, both of which came into use as aids to the unskilled in taking off the profiles of hills, valleys and buildings. Probably the most triumphantly successful use of the camera obscura in the making of prints is to be seen in the first states of Girtin's *Views of Paris*. Curiously, but quite logically, you have to be a much more accomplished draughtsman to make a good lively drawing with the aid of a camera of any kind than without it.

The attempts to make printed pictures with tints had begun early in the sixteenth century, as can be seen in a few prints by such artists as Marc Antonio and Daniel Hopfer. But these attempts were sporadic and had little consequence until the middle of the seventeenth century, when the first mezzotints were made. This method had a few followers in Holland and Germany. It was never popular in France, possibly because the typical French palette was high in key. But in England, where the palette was lower, mezzotinting became the standard British way of reproducing the portraits and fancy subjects of the day. Great skill was devoted to its practice and refinement, but it had a comparatively short life, and by the middle of the nineteenth century it had become antiquated. Curiously it was never used by a great artist as a medium for original work. Although Turner did all the work on a few of the plates for his *Liber Studiorum*, it is practically impossible to see any material difference between them and the plates in the same set that were done by the professional mezzotinters. The last brilliant flare-up of the mezzotint may be seen in the small prints that Constable, in the 1820's and 1830's, paid Lucas to make after small rough sketches which he furnished for the purpose. Constable corrected the proofs of the many states, and in so doing introduced so many and such great changes that it is fair to say that the impressions should be called original prints and not reproductive prints. There can be few documents of greater interest to anyone who desires to watch the artist's mind at work, than a well-selected series of the trial proofs of a number of these Lucas-Constable prints.

The trouble with all these ways of working on the copper was that copper is a very soft metal, and even under the hands of the most experienced and skilful of printers wears out with extravagant speed. This was especially true of the processes in which the surface of the plate was broken up very finely, as was necessary for the making of tints and tones. Books illustrated in these ways could only be printed in comparatively small and expensive editions which could not reach the general public. In many instances, such as that of the *Microcosm of London*, the letter press of the entire edition was printed at one time, and the plates were reworked and printed off from time to time as the book sold, so that the illustrations sometimes bear watermarks of many years later date than that which appears on the title pages. It would seem that most of the copies of Blake's *Songs of Innocence*, the pages of which were painted up by hand, were only made after orders had been received for them. It is to be remembered that the illustrations which have become part of the visual heritage of the general public —those in such books, for example, as Dürer's *Apocalypse*, the Florentine *Epistole e Evangelii*, and, in England, *Alice in Wonderland*—have always been printed from relief blocks which could be locked up with type in the printer's formes and run off in repeated and enormous editions.

A few technical experiments, for they cannot be called more than that, were made in Holland in the seventeenth century and in England in the middle of the eighteenth century, towards some method of producing relief blocks that would yield prints with adequate detail and tonality and at the same time produce large editions. But, practically, they came to nothing. Everywhere, however, the old techniques for making relief blocks on wood or soft metal had survived, principally for use as decorations for popular chap-books, song sheets, trade cards, and advertisements. The only large-scale original woodcuts of any artistic quality I recall in the eighteenth century were the two lone folio size woodcuts that Hogarth designed. Looking at them today we can see their power and colourful effectiveness, but their contemporaries had little use for them and Hogarth never repeated the experiment. They inspired no more interest or emulation than had the few and remarkably handsome woodcuts after Rubens in the first half of the seventeenth century.

In England the relief techniques survived in the shops where they made trade cards, coats of arms, emblems, bill heads, headings for ballads, and coarse-textured pictures for penny children's books. It was in one of these shops that Bewick served his apprenticeship and later was a partner. It is impossible to say when or where the discovery was made that the engraving tool could be used on a wooden block the surface of which ran at right angles to the grain of the wood instead of parallel with it. The method seems to have been in use in the shop in which Bewick worked. It remained for him to discover that it made possible the production from wood-blocks of lines that for practical purposes were as fine and as closely laid as those that were customarily laid on copper in any of the ordinary commercial processes of engraving and etching. More than that it made possible the production of tints, of black lines on white grounds, and of white lines on either tints or black grounds. The wood-blocks were capable of yielding very large editions. Nothing of this kind had been known before. Bewick made a number of publications which had but little effect on the public, but finally in 1797 he put forth the first volume of a popular ornithology, which he both wrote and illustrated, and that contained a great many anecdotal tail pieces which immediately captured the public attention by their salty, rural sentimentality. Bewick's *British Birds* may be said to have wagged their way into fame with their tail-pieces. The story of the development of this technique under the hands of Bewick and others constitutes a very important part of the story of prints during the nineteenth century. It brought the wood-block back into books, and gave the greater public for the first time copious illustration for its texts.

Almost simultaneously with Bewick's publication of the *British Birds*, there appeared the *Songs of Innocence*, written and illustrated by William Blake, and the *Caprichos* of Francisco Goya. The *Songs of Innocence* were printed from relief etchings on copper. The *Caprichos* were the first set of original and powerful works of art to be made in aquatint. Disregarding the artistic qualities of these two polarly different masterpieces of imaginative picture-making, the importance of their techniques did not emerge until long afterwards, and then in connection with processes of photo-mechanical reproduction of which no one in their time had ever dreamed. During the same years in which these three books or sets of pictures were being made, Aloys Senefelder, in Bavaria, was working out his discovery of a totally new graphic process, using completely novel materials and methods, and producing a kind of print that was absolutely unprecedented. Lithography is the only great historic graphic process of which we know the name of the inventor. What is even more remarkable is that he worked out most of the technical capabilities of the medium even as we have it today. Here at last was a graphic process in which the only person who had to have a technical training in process was the printer—for literally anyone who could make marks with either a pen or a pencil could, with the services of the printer, make a lithograph. Granted the ability to draw it was no longer necessary for anyone to study the handling of a highly artificial linear or other technique in order to make a printing surface. It was not necessary for the draughtsman who made the lithograph ever to have been in a lithographic establishment, ever to have seen a lithographic printing press, or even to have seen one of the stones from which the prints were pulled, for he could draw at choice directly on the stone or on paper, with a pencil, a pen, a crayon, or a brush, provided only that the pigment that came from it was greasy. I have myself, in a demonstration, made a print from a drawing that I made on a stone with a lipstick borrowed from a lady in the audience. Once his drawing was made, all the artist had to do was to hand it to the printer, who did the rest. But all this only came out in the nineteenth century.

Senefelder's discovery did two very remarkable things. It freed the original artist or draughtsman from the tyranny of the reproductive engraver's nets of rationality, and it enabled the public for the first time in many generations to get direct first hand exactly repeatable pictorial statements about things seen and imagined that could be printed in practically unlimited editions. The reign of second-hand visual information was drawing to its close.

Only five years after Senefelder made his discovery Wedgwood got a print by the action of light on a piece of chemically sensitized paper. Never before in all the history of the techniques of the repeatable picture had so many things of such vital importance been worked out in so short a time.

As we look back over the book illustration and the informational prints of the seventeenth and the eighteenth centuries, it becomes apparent that with very few exceptions they were pictures which were at one and two removes from the visual statements made by their titular makers. This is but another way of saying that the printing surfaces from which the illustrations and prints were struck off were not made by the draughtsmen or illustrators but by copyists of their drawings. In many instances, such as the reproductions of paintings and statues, the objects reproduced were copied by some draughtsman, and his drawing was then copied by the engraver, who did not work directly from the original work of art. The situation had implicit in it all the difficulties of which Pliny talked in his account of the Greek botanists.

We are apt to forget how long into the nineteenth century this situation persisted. Thus, for example, Walter Crane was sent to study drawing in an engraver's shop so that he would be able to make drawings that the engravers could understand and translate into their lines with the least difficulty.

The most that anyone looking at one of these engravings could hope for was that the broad general scheme of the composition was indicated in a generally adequate way, and that the iconographic detail was more or less truthful. The print never conveyed any information about the surface of the original or the manner in which it was worked. I may perhaps make my point in another way—if there were several paintings of the same general composition and incident, and there were engravings available of each of these paintings, no study of the prints could possibly determine which of them represented the original and which the copies or adaptations.

The well-known statue of the Laocoon was excavated early in the sixteenth century. It was engraved, etched, and cut on wood, at frequent intervals by different men, some of whom had seen the original, some of whom worked from drawings specially made for the purpose, and some by men who worked at first or second hand from prints that had previously been made. A group of these prints is here reproduced in chronological order from the 1520's to the 1890's, either enlarged or reduced so that the head of Laocoon is the same size in each. Each engraver, of course, phrased such information as he conveyed about it in terms of the net of rationality of his style of engraving. There is such a disparity between the visual statements they made that only by an effort of historical imagination is it possible to realize that all the so dissimilar pictures were supposed to tell the truth about the one identical thing. At best there is a vague family resemblance between them. Had they represented butterflies instead of a known single statue, one would have said that they represented different families of the genus Laocoonidae. A comparison of them immediately raises Pilate's question. It is easy to see that here we have posed as a practical matter one of the most difficult and abstruse problems known to the epistemologists.

When we think that it was on engravings of this kind that the comparison and discussion of the qualities and relative merits of works of art was based, it becomes easy to understand why so little of the art criticism and discussion of the past has any value for us of today, except in so far as it throws light on the thought of its times, and why the subjects about which the critics and theorists talked, the qualities they looked for and found or did not find in works of art, are so amusing and puzzling to us of today. The predicament was not peculiar to works of art, for it was inherent in every sort of visual information about everything in the world.

Thus whenever we read a book, especially about art, archaeology, or aesthetic theory, written prior to about the beginning of the first world war, it is well to ask ourselves to what extent the writer had both a dependable memory and a first hand acquaintance with the objects he referred to, to what extent he knew them through reproductions, and what sort of reproductions he depended on. Perhaps the most pregnant remark in Bosanquet's standard *History of Aesthetic,* is hidden in a short footnote which points out that when Lessing wrote about the Laocoon and expression in art he had never seen the original and probably depended for his visual knowledge of it upon engravings. It would have been difficult for Bosanquet, whose book was published in 1892 at a time when photography and the photo-mechanical processes were still in their infancy, to be aware of what he had done in his casual footnote, but when he had fired that one shot he had utterly wrecked most of the biggest tanks in the armies of eighteenth- and nineteenth-century connoisseurship and aesthetics.

There is an old and well-known French proverb and pun— *Que c'est meilleur d'être raisonnable que d'avoir raison*—which can only be translated by forgetting about the pun and saying that it is better to be reasonable than right.

When it came to things and objects about which they had no

immediate first-hand acquaintance and for information about which they had to rely on words and the available printed pictures —e.g. Goethe showing his engravings to Eckermann—the people of the eighteenth and most of the nineteenth century could only be reasonable, for it was utterly impossible for them to be right. They had not the means available to think in particularities, which are always irrational, and they had to think in generalities. Thus it came about that they thought their generalities were true, and that when observations did not agree with the generalities it was the observations that were wrong. To a very considerable extent they were still in the situation and the frame of mind that had caused the Greeks to think as they did about some of the basic problems in philosophy. Thus just as the ancient Greeks developed the Platonic doctrine of Ideas and Aristotle's essences, so the eighteenth century developed the ideas of the Truth of Science and of the Laws of Nature. It did this very largely because it was impossible for it to state exactly the particulars it saw in such a way that the statement could be verified. It was impossible for it to make and publish a pictorial statement that could not be challenged for its accuracy. Also it was impossible for it to make another pictorial statement about the same thing that should be like one that had already been made. In other words, it was impossible to verify any qualitative visual information except by going to where the thing was and looking at it, and when this was done the information was never accurate. An experiment leading up to visual recognitions of identity could be exactly repeated, but it might just as well not have been, for there was no way of stating the result of either experiment in such a way that the reports were either exact or exactly alike. All the eighteenth century could do with the pictorial means available to it was to take a series of visual statements and draw a sort of statistical average of what they contained. But no statistical average has ever existed in nature as a concrete fact. The moment we begin to think in terms of averages we confess that we have lost contact with the concrete things from which the average is calculated.

91

# THE TYRANNY OF THE RULE

Today we talk very little about either the 'Laws of Nature' or the 'Truth of Science', and, if we know what we are doing, we hold them in no very great respect, for we know that it is our business to challenge them, and that if we can find even a single instance in which a so-called law of nature does not work, that law will have to be recast, and that it is we who shall have to recast it. It is rather comic to think of a mere human being either making or recasting so august a thing as a law of nature, but that is just what he does. This is a very recent notion, and it has come about very largely through our experience with visual information and statements. An example is provided by the photographs of an eclipse that were taken in 1919 in Brazil and the Gulf of Guinea, which verified Professor Einstein's hypothesis about the action of gravitation on light. No man until very modern times could have produced a picture that would have been accepted as evidence that light was subject to gravitation. Similarly the photographs taken in the Cavendish Laboratory of vapour condensations in cloud chambers were accepted as evidence that the atom, instead of being simple, was exceedingly complex. Between them these two sets of photographs called for the complete recasting of what for several hundred years had been regarded as Laws of Nature, and involved such a radical overturn of basic notions as had probably never before happened in the history of thinking man.

# V

# THE TYRANNY BROKEN

# THE NINETEENTH CENTURY

With the nineteenth century we come to a period in which the printed picture may be said to have come of age. Not only did it use all the older processes but it invented more new ones than had been known in all previous history. I imagine that the number of printed pictures produced between 1800 and 1901 was probably considerably greater than the total number of printed pictures that had been produced before 1801. They were made for all classes of society and for every conceivable purpose. By the end of the century the exactly repeatable pictorial statement had become a commonplace in books, in periodicals, and in the daily newspapers. It was spread on exterior walls for advertising and propaganda, and on interior ones for decoration. It had become an absolute necessity in manufacture and engineering of every variety. The most important single development in the century was the discovery and exploitation of photography and photographic process. First it eliminated the draughtsman, and then it eliminated the engraver from the making of exactly repeatable pictorial statements, and after that it went on to develop ways of repeating such statements in unlimited quantities. Such statements were no longer confined to the life of a single printing surface.

As the community became engulfed in printed pictures, it looked to them for most of its visual information. Even museum experts who have the original works of art at hand are apt to make their comparisons by juxtaposing photographic reproductions rather than by placing the originals side by side. As people became habituated to absorbing their visual information from photographic pictures printed in printers' ink, it was not long before this kind of impersonal visual record had a most marked effect on what the community thought it saw with its own eyes. It began to see photographically, it stopped talking about photographic distortion, and finally it adopted the photographic image as the norm of truthfulness in representation. A faith was put in the photograph that had never been and could not be put in the older hand-made pictures. There have been many revolutions in thought and philosophy, in science and religion, but I believe that never in the history of men has there been a more complete revolution than that which has taken place since the middle of the nineteenth century in seeing and visual recording. Photographs give us visual evidence about things that no man has ever seen or ever will see directly. A photograph is today accepted as proof of the existence of things and shapes that never would have been believed on the evidence of a hand-made picture. The nineteenth century began by believing that what was reasonable was true and it wound up by believing that what it saw a photograph of was true—from the finish of a horse race to the nebulae in the sky. The photograph has been accepted as showing that impossible desideratum of the historian—*wie es eigentlich gewesen*—how it actually was.

At the end of the eighteenth century there were several remarkable innovations in the graphic techniques and those that were utilized to make their materials. Bewick developed the method of using engraving tools on the end of the wood. Senefelder discovered lithography. Blake made relief etchings. Early in the nineteenth century Stanhope, Clymer, Koenig, and others introduced new kinds of type presses, which for strength surpassed anything that had previously been known. Koenig's machine not only was operated by power instead of human muscle, but its mechanical design required a complete change in the methods of inking the printing surfaces, which in turn necessitated an abandonment of the ancient practice of lowering the faces of the blocks and the substitution for it of the system of overlays. Photography, although the first tentative steps towards it were taken in the eighteenth century, did not play any important role until the middle of the century, after which it brought about a catastrophic revolution, the extent of which is not even today fully recognized.

For a long time the traditional graphic techniques of the copper continued to be used. They held their heads bravely against the newer processes until about the middle of the century, when their inability to compete against the younger methods began to tell against them. For a while, after that, they maintained their existence through the snobbery of a tradition of the best, but long before the end of the century they had definitely entered upon decline towards the atrophy which has ultimately overtaken them. Today the old style line engraving, mezzotint, and reproductive etching, have for all practical purposes ceased to exist. The various forms of etching lead a precarious existence among artists who happen to like them as media for the exhibition of their skill and deftness in hallowed techniques, and there are still collectors who take an interest in the current production of minor works of art in antiquated and therefore highly respectable techniques. But, as a medium that still has work to do in the world, etching, aside from its utilization in the photographic processes, is over with. Today it has no more social or economic importance than has the ability to drive a four in hand in front of a coach. Wood-engraving and woodcutting are in much the same straits as etching and engraving. All have become precious—accomplishments of which their practitioners are vain—much like the acquisition of a good French accent by one who has nothing to say in any language.

In thinking about all this it is worth while to reflect upon the fact that with a very few remarkable exceptions the greater artistic single sheet prints since the end of the first quarter of the sixteenth century have been made in techniques which at the time were currently and familiarly used for utilitarian purposes and especially for the illustration of books.

If we stop at eighteen hundred and look back at the prints that had been made up to that time, one of the outstanding characteristics of the movement represented in them seems to have been a gradual withdrawal from print making by the more important artists. In the fourteen-hundreds we find such masters as Pollaiuolo and Mantegna, Schongauer and the young Dürer, making prints with their own hands. In the fifteen-hundreds the list of important painters who made prints with their own hands is very large—the mature Dürer, Holbein, Altdorfer, Cranach, Lucas of Leyden, Titian, Parmigiano, Baroccio, Spagnoletto, among others. In the sixteen-hundreds among the men who made prints with their own hands were Rembrandt, Van Dyck, Ruysdael, Claude le Lorrain, Guido Reni, Guercino, Carlo Maratti, and many more. Rubens made only one or two etchings with his own hands, but he exercised immediate supervision over the prints that he published after his own paintings, proof reading and correcting them until they met with his approval. In the next century, however, the eighteenth, we discover that of the major French artists, Watteau made only six or seven immaterial sketches on the copper, and Fragonard a handful of charming little prints of no particular importance. In England Hogarth made many plates after his own pictures,—perhaps the last instance in which a major artist consistently did reproductive work. In Italy the only outstanding painters to etch were Canaletto and the elder Tiepolo, and their etched work is small in volume. Piranesi was a commercial manufacturer of architectural prints— conveyors of information—and but rarely let his genius interfere with his business. Only in Spain did a great and powerful painter turn to etching and aquatint for the expression of ideas that he had not previously given to the world in paint. If Goya had been in

57. Portion of a wood-engraving of a drawing after Giotto, from *Arena Chapel, Padua*, 1860. About actual size.

58. Wood-engraving of Holman Hunt's drawing of 'The
Lady of Shalott', from the pre-Raphaelite *Tennyson* of
1857. About actual size.

*From W. Holman Hunt to his good Wife Edith Marion. 1881*

59. Reproduction of a collotype from a photograph of
Hunt's original drawing on the block.
About actual size.

60. Portion of a relief print in the Comte process, by Charles Jacque. Presumably in the 1870's. About actual size.

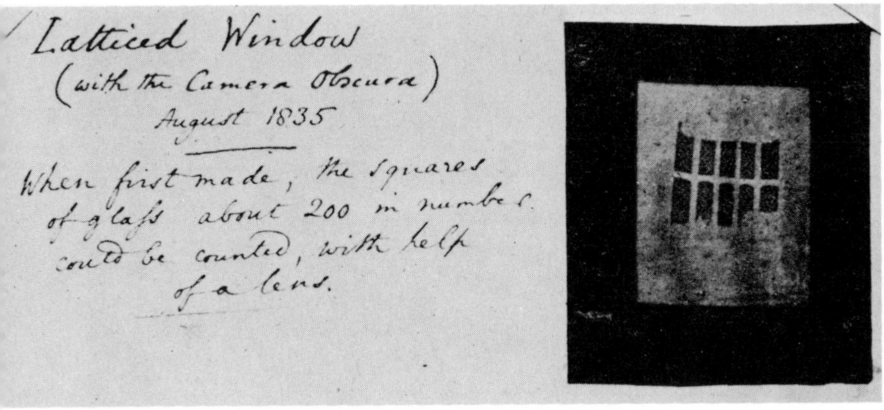

Latticed Window
(with the Camera Obscura)
August 1835

When first made, the squares
of glass about 200 in number
could be counted, with help
of a lens.

61. Photograph of a Latticed Window at Lacock Abbey made by Fox Talbot in August, 1835. About actual size.

62. Flaxman's relief 'Deliver us from Evil', as engraved by Bolton through a photograph on the woodblock. About 1861. About actual size.

63. Head from an old drawing, as engraved by Linton through a photograph on the woodblock. Enlarged.

64. Portion of a pen lithograph, by Stothard, from the *Polyautographic Album* of 1803. Enlarged.

France or Italy it is to be doubted whether he would have broken away from the accepted code of procedure and himself done important work in etching, but, as it was, there was no competent school of engravers in Spain to intervene between him and his public. He had to do the work with his own hands. Provinciality and ignorance sometimes have a great deal to do with originality.

To translate these facts into other terms, the world during the eighteenth century had ceased to receive first hand exactly repeatable pictorial statements or communications from its most important artists. What it got were second- and third-hand statements of hearsay evidence. The same thing was true of the illustrations in its books.

Thanks to the introduction of economies and notions of business efficiency in the engravers' shops there had become universal the practice of splitting up among various hands the different steps in the making of exactly repeatable pictorial statements. At the end of the chain stood the original draughtsman or painter. Then came the draughtsman for the engraver. Frequently at this point came a specialist who made the preliminary etching on the plate. And finally came the engraver himself, who in many instances had never seen the original of which he was supposed to make a reproduction, and who rarely hesitated to correct what he considered the poor drawing or the lack of elegance in the copy that lay before him. In the addenda at the end of the 1861 edition of Jackson and Chatto's *History of Wood-engraving* there is a defence of this latter procedure. Rossetti's wails of anguish over the way that the Dalziel engraving shop corrected his drawings for Tennyson are famous among people who are interested in Victorian English poetry.

This subdivision of labour, although, as we have seen, it began in the sixteenth century, was perhaps carried further in the peculiarly nineteenth century medium of wood-engraving than in any other. At the risk of mixing up my chronological account I shall deal for a moment with something that did not come about

97

in its fully developed state until the beginning of the second half of the nineteenth century.

In wood-engraving it became the standard practice to have a draughtsman make a drawing of a painting or whatever it was of which a picture was wanted. Then this drawing was redrawn on the engraver's block by a specialist draughtsman who was supposed to know how a drawing should be made for an engraver— even though in many instances this secondary draughtsman had never seen the original. Only then did the engraver begin his work. I recall one instance in which the final engraving was done by at least four different engravers, each according to his speciality of landscapes, figures, architecture, skies, etc. I have no doubt that there were many more instances of this kind of thing. The individual engravers no longer signed their work, which bore the name of the shop in which the blocks were turned out. In France the engraver continued to sign his work long after he had ceased to do so in England.

This subdivision of specialized skill was carried to its final limit of economic practicability and artistic and reportorial folly in the big double page wood-engravings that appeared in the popular weekly papers of the middle of the century. To show how this worked: The artists in the field or at the front would send back little sketches of the most generalized and undetailed variety. These were then copied in large size on the big blocks for the centre pages by draughtsmen attached to the home offices, who supplied the detail and the tonality missing in the little sketches. During the Crimean War Constantin Guys was the field artist of the *Illustrated London News*, and his little drawings were blown up by Gavarni in London. The big blocks were made by clamping together many little pieces of wood. In America, when the final drawing had been made on the block, the clamps were removed from the block, it was disassembled, and each piece was given to a different engraver in a quantity production shop. Each engraver then engraved the middle of the surface of his piece of the big block, while carefully leaving untouched a little margin about his work. When the little

98

pieces of wood had been treated in this way they were reassembled and clamped together again, after which the big block went to a particularly skilled engraver whose task it was to knit the picture together by engraving the untouched margins of the little pieces in such a way that their joins would not be too strikingly noticeable. The result was only what might have been expected. In the first place, all the engravers had to engrave as much alike as possible, using a predetermined system or network of engraved lines in which they had been trained. The prints from the big blocks were thus second- or third- or fourth-hand accounts, or even badly jumbled accounts by many different people, of what things were supposed to look like. Not only was there no impersonal state-ment such as was later to be supplied by the camera, but there was no first-hand statement at all. The responsibility for pictorial statements had been by-passed, and such statements as were actually made had been reduced to a flat dull plane of reason-ability.

Under the circumstances, no faith could be put in any exactly repeated pictorial statement of fact beyond what might seem to be within the realm of general common sense and reasonability of people who literally knew nothing at first-hand and who had never seen a first-hand statement of what was being stated. Any-thing that to them seemed unreasonable, or as they used to say in New England 'agin Natur', or mixed up or unclear, was suspect. When a report of what happens in the Hindu Kush has to be made in such a way as to appear reasonable to persons who have never been more than forty miles from St. Paul's the report will bear very little resemblance to the fact. I personally have little doubt that this rationalized and untrustworthy hearsay visual evidence had a great deal to do with the seventeenth and eighteenth cen-turies' general demand for reasonability. I am certain that it had much to do with the prevailing lack of imagination in eighteenth century art and literature and the dominance in them of varieties of common sense. If there had been hand cameras in the days when Boswell took Dr. Johnson on that trip to the Hebrides, no one would have thought that he should take his diary of the trip to Malone to have its sharp notation of details excised and its place taken by common sense generalities.

In the first half of the nineteenth century the technique of etching and of mixed etching and engraving, especially at the hands of such men as reproduced the drawings and paintings of Turner, was carried to such a state of technical surety and expertness as had never before and has not since been equalled. It is one of the greater ironies that the much touted Revival of Etching, which the books tell us began about the middle of the nineteenth century, was actually not a revival of the craft of etching at all but the adoption of the technique by a group of on the whole rather poor draughtsmen and incompetent technicians who in one way or another managed to gain the attention of the public. In a period, like that of the 1890's, in which Whistler was often said, and by many believed, to be the greatest etcher since Rembrandt, it was easy to forget not only the work of such masters of technique as the Findens, but the very existence of such great draughtsmen on the copper as Piranesi, Canaletto, Goya, Delacroix and his fellow romantics, and of such Englishmen as Hogarth, Rowlandson, Girtin, and Cotman. It was also distressingly easy to overlook the etchings of such contemporaries as Manet and Degas. The emphasis on etching as such was an escape from the problem of draughtsmanship and design. When a man asks do you not think this is a good etching, his words relate to the craft and not to the picture—an inversion of interest and importances that has fooled a great many innocent people. It is a hang over from the eighteenth century's interest in the moiré of engraved lines and its forgetfulness of the picture.

Original line engraving produced but two still generally recognized masters during the nineteenth century—Blake and Gaillard —the one a very incompetent technician and draughtsman, the other a portraitist of the type exemplified in oil paint by Balthazar Denner. Blake, who was born in 1757, based his style on the prints by the weaker stylizing followers of Marc Antonio and was completely out of sympathy with the point of view of such a man as Rembrandt. It is to be noted that the appreciation of Blake's work has been confined in largest measure to persons of bookish tastes rather than of visual tastes and experiences, and that it has never extended beyond the boundaries of the English speaking peoples. When considered in connection with the comparative poverty of those peoples in the arts of design, this last fact has implications of great interest. Gaillard was one of the leaders in a belated French mid-century revolt against the tyranny of the traditional lozenge and dot structure in line engraving. His ideal would seem to have been a sort of hand-made daguerreotype, and his linear structure got below the threshold of what for most persons is the limit of unaided eyesight. Many people had, and, alas, still have, the notion that the more niggling lines an etcher or engraver can lay in a given space the more remarkable a technician he is. It is perilously easy to forget that after all an etching or engraving is a drawing and that the most important thing in a drawing is draughtsmanship. Line engraving may be said to have met its Waterloo with the invention of a method of engraving on steel for the making of bank notes. With this it took little time for it to become a trade and not an art.

The two most interesting developments of the first half of the nineteenth century took place in wood-engraving and in lithography. Wood-engraving was carried to its greatest and silliest peaks of virtuosity in England—a country that never took kindly to lithography even though it used a great deal of it for menial purposes. I have a friend whose opinions are much like those of the late Queen Victoria—you can count on him to express what most Englishmen thought seventy-five years ago. He tells me that a lithograph has no character and is merely a reproduction of a drawing, and is therefore not comparable to an etching or engraving, which has an exquisite artistic character no matter how dull it may be. In any event, lithography received its greatest development in France, which also made great use of wood-engraving, though never in the pedantic manner that delighted the English. It may be that if I had been born and educated in Central Europe I should find the German and Austrian graphic output of the nineteenth century of more interest and significance than I do. Unless I am horribly mistaken the only artistically worthwhile prints made in Germany during the greater part of the century were those that came out of the printing office of the *Fliegende Blaetter* and other such irreverent and unsolemn places.

The development of the Bewickian wood-engraving in England is interesting for reasons other than its minor artistic merits. It provides a typical case history of what happens when a new process or technique is introduced and is not rapidly put to use by men of genius. It is particularly valuable because the material is copious and the data are in general easily accessible. The prime factors involved, in addition to the finely reticulated surface of the wood-block, were the paper, the ink, the method of inking the block, and the press. Except for several minor innovations in the design of the press, these things had remained without material change from the fourteen-hundreds until about 1800, and on the continent of Europe did so until a generation later. It was the insistent demand for the new wood engravings that caused all these things to undergo the great changes that took place in them by the middle of the century. William Morris and his typographical followers have finely damned all the works of that period, forgetting that they themselves were among them. But, much influence as the Morris doctrine has had in certain limited and snobbish sorts of printing, the facts remain that our modern techniques and our modern requirements come out of what may be called the Bewickian revolution. It is to be noted that the final test of the technical skill of the pressman is to be looked for in how cleanly he prints his fine textured blocks and half tones and not in how much ink he can load on his types.

Bewick, in the eighteenth century, had been able to secure good impressions from his blocks—which were not comparable in fineness of texture to our ordinary half tones—but only by rubbing the paper down onto the inked blocks with an engraver's burnisher. Moreover he had been able to secure excellent impressions only by using little pieces of the yellowish, very smooth, and very thin paper with which at that time the Chinese packed their shipments of tea to England. The impressions of his blocks which appeared in 1797, in the first edition of the first volume of his *British Birds*, were actually so poor that in 1800, in response to popular demand, he issued a volume containing impressions of them printed on one side of the paper only and without text. When we of today look at these impressions of 1800, the first thing we are aware of is the exceedingly poor quality of the prints from the blocks. Much of the detail is literally illegible. No newspaper of today, running off its edition of half a million copies in a few hours, would tolerate what Bewick in 1800 thought good. It was not until towards the end of his life that Bewick was able to secure a supply of India or China paper sufficient in quantity to run off a very small edition de luxe of impressions from the blocks of the *British Birds* which really showed what was in them.

In 1809 there was published a slender volume of text and wood-engravings under the title *Religious Emblems, Being a Series of Engravings on Wood . . . from Designs drawn on the Blocks Themselves by J. Thurston Esq.*, some copies of which had the peculiarity that the text was printed on book paper while the blocks were separately struck off on sheets of China paper that were then bound up in appropriate places between the text pages. In 1810 a small number of copies of Rogers's *Pleasures of Memory* was issued in which both the text and the wood-engravings, by Clennell after Stothard, were printed on very thin smooth China paper. I can recall no earlier instance of either practice, that used in the *Emblems* or that used in the *Pleasures*, both of which have become well-known ways of giving a snobbish appeal to picture books, usually of minor artistic interest. The engravings in the *Emblems* were rather elaborate essays in the production of tones extending from light greys to the fullest blacks. Those in the *Pleasures* were called facsimiles of line drawings. The quality of the prints in these two volumes is far better than any that Bewick was ever able to produce in his regularly issued volumes.

In 1817 there was a limited edition of *Puckle's Club*, in which the remarkably fine textured illustrations—far finer than any that had previously been produced—were struck off on thin China or India paper that was mounted on the text pages. The equally fine textured tail pieces were printed directly on the paper used in the text, and much of their work vanished because the lines of the blocks were so much finer than the texture of the paper.

In 1822 there appeared Savage's *Hints on Decorative Printing*, a very de luxe effort, which contained, in addition to many costly experiments in colour printing, two of the most amazing and remarkably foolish emulations or adaptations of copper plate techniques to engraving on wood that have ever been made. They were printed on China paper mounted down, and were accompanied by impressions from the cancelled blocks carefully printed on the paper used for the type pages. The difference between the impressions on the two sorts of paper is striking. So far as I recall this is the first book in which impressions from the cancelled printing surfaces of the illustrations were included. A mere trick of snobbery in this instance serves a useful end for the student of techniques.

In 1824, what was perhaps the apogee of the search for fineness of black line linear texture was reached in Henderson's *History of Ancient and Modern Wines*, the head-pieces and initials in which also had to be printed on India paper that was mounted on the regular paper of the text. Here again it is possible to see the difference made by the paper, for Bohn reprinted many of the blocks on good smooth paper of a commercial variety in his edition of Jackson and Chatto's *History* of *Wood-engraving*. After the Henderson very few attempts were made to rival on wood the fineness of the etched or engraved lines on copper. The cost of printing, and the difficulty of procuring the proper exotic paper, made it impossible to supply the greater public with illustrated books of this kind. Wood-engraving, like type printing, was not to come of age until it had come down from the higher levels of expensiveness and become a rather cheap and common thing.

The one way in which these wonderful but silly books resembled each other was that, even when their illustrations were supposed to be facsimiles of pen or pencil lines, they smelled to Heaven of engraving. The Rogers of 1810 was long famous for the accuracy with which it reproduced the quality of Stothard's lines, and remained so until after the pervasion of the photomechanical processes. As we look at its illustrations today their outstanding quality comes from the fact that their lines are engraved and reek of the engraver's tool.

Bewick, if not a great artist, was a very original one with a good deal to say of an amusing anecdotal kind. His sketches were no more than preliminary studies for the finished engravings that came from his hand, with their free, bold, and often brilliant representations of textures. The one way in which his prints differ technically from all previous woodcuts and engravings on copper is that the linear structure is sometimes in black lines on white grounds and sometimes in white lines on black grounds. Otherwise they have the same kind of a net of rationality, although a different one, as the earlier prints. The other two original wood-engravers of the first part of the century in England, Blake and Calvert, had much the same technical approach as Bewick, but modified in practice by their so different personalities and interests. They were more interested in making their statements than in exhibiting their mere virtuosity in the use of the engraver's tool. But this cannot be said of many of their contemporaries and followers, for whom their engraving was of much more importance than the drawings on the blocks. Even when, as in the case of Harvey, they made the drawings they engraved, the final result was of much more interest as a *tour de force* of engraving than it was as a design. As early as 1821 the idea had grown up for wood-engraving, just as it had long before for copper engraving, that a wood-engraving should look like a wood-engraving and be all neat and tidy with its net of lines.

105

We find this clearly stated in the footnote at the beginning of the first Eclogue in Thornton's *Vergil*, of 1821, where Thornton says, 'The Illustrations of this English Pastoral are by the famous Blake, the Illustrator of Young's *Night Thoughts*, and Blair's *Grave*; who designed and engraved them himself. This is mentioned, as they display less of art than genius, and are much admired by some eminent painters.' Thornton did not think to mention that in his horror at genius as distinct from art he had had a number of Blake's blocks remade by other more routine hands, in such a way that they would be more 'artistic'. I recall no other instance in which we get so clear a verbal statement of the tyranny of the standardized network of the engraved line, but if we use our eyes we can find many others with great ease.

Harvey, after working with Bewick as an apprentice, transferred to the studio of B. R. Haydon, the painter, there to learn drawing—in itself a commentary upon many things. While with Haydon he copied Haydon's painting of the 'Death of Lucius Quintus Dentatus' on what was then considered an enormous block, for it was 15 by $11\frac{1}{2}$ inches in size. He finished the block after having worked at it for much of three years, and then, to his chagrin, discovered that there was no printing press in England powerful enough to produce a proper impression of it. It was not until the early 1820's that Johnson, the printer, discovered that the Columbian Press, then but recently introduced into England by Clymer of Philadelphia, when rigged with a much lengthened bar and operated by two strong men instead of a single boy, was strong enough to print Harvey's block. Johnson's account of this incident and his account of the other presses then in use in England, as given in his *Typographia* of 1824, are of prime interest to anyone curious about the problems presented by the new graphic technique. Incidentally, Johnson had to work out a new printer's ink that would be both thin enough and opaque enough for the printing of Harvey's block. From that time on the problem presented by the ink became a matter for serious thought, for it could no longer be coped with by the traditional recipes. In 1817 ink rollers were put on the market to take the place of the ink balls that had been in use since the fifteenth century.

It soon became evident that the greater public, while it had little interest in the virtuosity of the wood-engravers or in wood-engraving as such, was very much interested in pictorial information at a small price. Thus it may be that the most important event in the middle history of wood-engraving in England was the founding by Charles Knight in 1832 of his weekly *Penny Magazine*. It was produced on a cylinder press, operated by steam, which raised the output of two men working eight hours a day from the 1,000 sheets reached by the old hand-operated press to 16,000 sheets printed on both sides. Within a year its circulation reached the astonishing number of 200,000. It owed much of its popularity to the fact that it was illustrated with coarse wood-engravings and was directed at a public which previously had been given but slight attention by the publishers of picture books. This public liked pictures and drawings and cared nothing about methods of reproduction. It was, therefore, not very long before the emphasis in the illustration of books shifted from the fact that the pictures were engravings to the fact that they were supposed to be facsimiles of drawings. The early illustrations of this kind were dull enough hack work, but finally in 1857 there appeared the affectionately remembered pre-Raphaelite *Tennyson*, full of illustrations drawn on the blocks by such men as Hunt, Millais and Rossetti. In that year there appeared the first number of *Once a Week*, which called to its service some remarkable pictorial talent.

About 1860, a minor wood-engraver, named Thomas Bolton, had the idea of sensitizing the surface of his wood-block, on which he had a photograph printed from a negative after a relief by Flaxman. He made his engraving through the photograph as though it had been a drawing in tints on the block. A print of it is to be found in the Jackson and Chatto *Treatise on Wood-engraving* in Bohn's edition, in which it was included as a novelty, but without any particular comment. So far as I have noticed it represented the first effective step towards that final substitution of photography for draughtsmanship in informative book illustration that could be printed at the same time as the text it accompanied. When we reach the page in the Jackson and Chatto which contains the impression from Bolton's block we seem to step into another world of vision, and for the first time to meet a repeatable pictorial statement in which we can have a little confidence. If we read our history backwards—which is the only way in which it can be read intelligently—this neglected little print by Bolton must be regarded as in many ways the most important wood-engraving that had been made up to its time. The history of the next forty years of book illustration is little more than an account of the pervasion of Bolton's idea, and its final development into the trivial, boring, and empty virtuosity of engraving over a photographic basis, that was, so short a time ago, the much vaunted characteristic of the American school of wood-engraving. It was displaced at the end of the century by a process of making photographic pictures in which even the engraver himself was dispensed with.

From the point of view of their artistic content, I have little doubt that the most remarkable wood-engravings of the nineteenth century were some of those for which the drawings on the blocks were made by Daumier in France.

Now to turn to the lithograph—Senefelder in his youth was a musical composer who had great difficulty in getting his music published, and who was too poor to pay for it himself. This turned his mind to the techniques of music printing. In the course of his thought about this he discovered, by an accident which involved a wash list, the principle on which lithography works. From being a poor musician he turned into an inventor and promoter. Unfortunately for him he could not get an effective patent and the first description of his process was made by someone else. However, within a few years his representatives and emulators were busy in many of the major cities of Europe. He made his discovery in 1797, and within the next year or so had himself introduced it into England. By 1803 the *Polyautographic Album* had been published in London. By the next year a similar publication under a

German version of the same name had been published in Berlin. Several French artists, notably Vivant Denon, learned lithography during the Napoleonic invasions of Germany, and, carrying the technique back to Paris, succeeded, after the Restoration, in getting the highest in the land to practise it as a diversion. In this he was undoubtedly helped by the fact that one of the earliest lithographic portraits had been made in England by the young refugee Duc de Montpensier of his brother who was later to become King Louis Philippe. In 1816, Engelmann, an Alsatian, set up a lithographic printing establishment in Paris.

In Germany and in England the new process had little luck in those it attracted to its use, and its possibilities lay dormant while second-rate and worse draughtsmen used it in imitation of timid drawings in pen and ink and in chalks. In 1807 in Germany it was used to produce copies of the pen drawings by Dürer for the Emperor Maximilian's prayer book, which was shortly followed by a long series of volumes devoted to the reproduction of paintings and drawings in famous collections. To put it mildly they were villainous libels. Also there were some drawing books in which misguided men attempted to show small boys and girls how they really ought not to draw. And there were a few timid romantic landscapes, and ruins, and old buildings. In England the *Album* of 1803 contained drawings by such men as Benjamin West and Stothard and a number of the lesser landscapists, but none of them shows that lithography had anything more in store than the reproduction of academic and timid pedantries. There are no artistically noteworthy English lithographs, and very few German ones.

In France, however, by 1825 there had come to the new process such men as Ingres, Géricault, and Delacroix. About that same year, Goya, from his retirement in southern France, broke forth with his famous set of four large lithographs of bull fights, to which he brought all his painter's bold draughtsmanship, and all his feeling for design, for colour, and for atmosphere. For those with the wit to understand, these prints were the declaration of independence of the new medium. He showed that it was made to the hand of the painter accustomed to draw with the brush and was not confined to the hands of the engraver craftsmen. In 1828 Delacroix illustrated Goethe's *Faust*. Its effect was like that of a bombshell. Paris was rapidly filled with practitioners of the new technique, among whom were many of the best painters of the day. In 1830 Philipon started the *Caricature*, which was followed in 1832 by the *Charivari*. Philipon began to publish Daumier's work early in the thirties, and, with one short interval in the middle of the century, his work continued to appear until 1871. Few of the French painters of the nineteenth century who achieved great and abiding renown did not at one time or another try their hands at lithography. A mere short list of some of them—Prudhon, Ingres, Decamps, Diaz, Géricault, Delacroix, Chasseriau, Daumier, Millet, Corot, Puvis, Manet, Degas, Cezanne, Pissarro, Renoir, Gauguin, Redon, and Toulouse-Lautrec—is sufficient. Alongside these painters there were professional makers of prints, as, for instance, Isabey and Raffet, Gavarni and Doré, who greatly affected public taste and thought. It is to be doubted whether any of all the mediums for making prints called to itself in so short a time such a group of great masters as made lithographs in Paris between 1825 and 1901.

The advantage of lithography was that the artist's drawing and the print were practically identical—there was no reworking of his drawing by another hand, let alone any copying of it in another medium, and it could be made in any way and with any or no linear scheme as the artist liked. It afforded the most complete gamut of tones between white and black, and achieved them with the greatest ease. A lithograph could be as loose and sketchy as Manet's 'Race Course', or as elaborately worked as Delacroix's 'Sister of Du Guesclin'—in other words it could do anything between the first roughest pencil or chalk sketch to something that can only be compared to a fully developed and detailed oil painting. It completely did away with any need for the translator-middle man-engraver with his inevitable systematized grammar and syntax of linear webbing. Its defect was that, like the copper-plate processes, it had to be printed in a different press than that which printed type, and thus called for two separate printings if it were to be used as a book illustration.

Many of Daumier's finest designs fell victims of an attempt to circumvent this double printing. He made his lithographs as usual, but they were transferred to metal plates and then bitten so that they could be printed as relief blocks with and at the same time as the text of the newspaper. As it was then impossible, in the short time at command, to prepare the 'make ready' required to bring out the colour values of the lines, these prints in the *Charivari* lost most of their colour and variety of tone. Little as print collectors may fancy them because of their lack of colour and that curious thing the collectors call 'quality', these quasi-lithographs number among them some of the most magisterial prints that Daumier ever made.

From the particular point of view here taken, it is interesting to notice that Daumier never became a professional lithographer and never made any prints to show his virtuosity in the medium in which he did most of his work. If I recall correctly he made but one reproductive print after another man's picture in all his life. He simply drew with the lithographic material on a piece of lithographic stone, and with it said what he had to say about life and politics, with never a thought that he should show off what tricks he could do with the medium. It is probable that in this he ranks with Mantegna, Titian, the old Rembrandt, Goya, and Degas, who so dominated their graphic processes that they gave them but little thought for what they might be in their own right, and certainly gave no thought to the notion that it is an artist's duty to stay within and to exploit what the community regards as the characteristic qualities of his medium.

Lithography's final flare-up took place in the last decade of the nineteenth century, when it was triumphantly used for a short while as the simplest and easiest medium in which to produce advertising posters, some of which were of enormous size. The great master of this episode was Toulouse-Lautrec.

It is amusing to notice that as the English and German speaking worlds have become acquainted with the graphic work of these French painters of the nineteenth century whose names I have mentioned—an acquaintanceship that hardly goes back of the first World War—the popularity of these prints by men who cared nothing about the traditional conventions for the dress and conduct of nice prints in society, has brought about a very remarkable change in taste and feeling about prints of all kinds. It has worked backwards and brought out into the light many earlier prints that were overlooked because they did not conform to the tricks and virtuosities which for generations had appealed to the 'graphic hearts and eyes' of the connoisseurs of the trivial qualities of mere manipulation. And it has caused many towering reputations, both of the long past and of yesterday, to take great falls. Not the least interesting part of this is that it has occurred simultaneously with the perfection of the modern techniques in photography and photographic process which have made adequate reproductions of the older prints both possible and common. The collectors, like the greater public, are finally discovering that what counts in original prints is pretty much the same thing that counts in painting and design, and not mere slickness in traditional rituals of technique. Someone said about Blaise Pascal that he had no style, he merely had important ideas which he expressed in such form that there was no difference between his words and his thought.

65. Portion of a lithograph of a Bull Fight, by Goya. About 1825. Reduced.

66. Portion of Delacroix's lithograph of 'La Sœur de Du Guesclin'.
About actual size.

67. Portion of Daumier's lithograph 'Un zeste! un rien!', from *Le Boulevard*.
Reduced.

68. Portion of Manet's lithograph after his painting of 'Les Courses'. About actual size.

69. Engraved illustration of a Roman wall painting, from Winckelmann's
*History of Ancient Art*, 1880. About actual size.

70. Line block after a pen drawing by Vierge, for *Pablo de Segovie*, 1881. About actual size.

71. Portion of a grain half-tone after a drawing by Natoire, from *L'Artiste*, 1882. Enlarged.

72. Portion of an early cross line half-tone after a photograph of a classical sculpture, from Furtwängler's *Meisterwerke der Griechischen Plastik*, 1893. Enlarged.

# VI

## PICTORIAL STATEMENT

## WITHOUT SYNTAX

## THE NINETEENTH CENTURY

D URING the nineteenth century there were a great many experiments and trials of novel technical ideas in print-making. Many of these techniques had appreciable merits from practical points of view, but inevitably most of them vanished very rapidly as still newer methods were introduced. In the lack of any extrinsic evidence it is frequently difficult if not impossible to tell from the face of a relief print made in the middle years of the century just what process was actually used in its making.

The adherents of the old traditional techniques, in their losing battle for supremacy, set up an idea which for a long time in-fluenced not only the critics but the general public. It was that, somehow, the old processes were intrinsically more artistic than the newer ones. In the print-collecting game there were purely verbalistic definitions of what was artistic that had nothing to do with either design or expression. Thus there gradually grew up in the public mind a notion that there was an artistic hierarchy of the graphic media. In the United States, for example, there was a strongly and generally held opinion that etching was more artistic than line-engraving, that both were more artistic than wood-engraving, that wood-engraving was more artistic than wood-cutting, and that all were more artistic than lithography. Lowest of all and utterly contemptible, were photography and any medium that bore the name of some 'process'.

I have, myself, been scolded by gentlemen of the older school for buying lithographs for my institution when I could have bought etchings for it, and for buying the horrid rough old woodcuts by such artists as Dürer and Cranach when I could have bought the charming, refined, and delicate, white line reproductive, wood-engravings of such modern masters as Timothy Cole and Elbridge Kingsley. Any so-called 'original' print by any minor artist was *per se* more artistic than one made under the supervision of even the greatest artist and after a design that he had made specially for the purpose. A well-known collector, famous for his artistic perception and taste, once took me severely to task for showing in the same exhibition prints from Turner's *Liber Studiorum* in which the work was all done by Turner himself and prints from the same series in which all the work on the plates was done by professional engravers working under Turner's immediate supervision. Later, when this doctrinaire had become very enthusiastic over some colour prints in an exhibition, I showed him that they were merely the front covers of an old French weekly journal, carefully matted so as to cover up their tell tale titles and type printing. Had he seen them first unmatted they would have been what in his estimation was the lowest of the low, mere process reproductions of drawings that had been specially made to be reproduced that way.

As we look back from the middle of the twentieth century all that kind of talk and opinion seems very silly, for it has become obvious that what makes a medium artistically important is not any quality of the medium itself but the qualities of mind and hand that its users bring to it.

Thus, there is doubtfully any more ungrateful medium than the now forgotten chalk plate, and yet it was probably the medium in which Daumier in the 1830's produced some of his more astonishing prints. In the middle of the century at Paris many of the best artists made prints by the various processes associated with the names of Gillot and of Comte. Because they were known, not as etchings, or engravings, or lithographs, but as the Comte process or the Gillot process, and because their results came out in popular books and magazines, they have been overlooked by the students of prints, although many of them were fully autographic, involved no use of photography, and were often of great interest and charm. Perhaps the funniest of these instances in which verbal definitions got in the way of eyesight and appreciation is provided by the *clichés verre* or *clichés glace*, which had a short vogue among such painters as Corot, Millet and Rousseau. After the invention of photographic paper that could be bought in packages, ready made and ready for use, these artists took to covering sheets of glass with a light resistant coating and then scratching or working a design through this, so that the glass could be used as a photographic negative from which photographic prints could be taken. So far as the artist was concerned it was a much more direct and simple process than etching. But because these prints were neither etchings, nor lithographs, and because they were not actually photographs made with a camera, they never became popular among collectors or public. People simply could not adjust themselves to such shocking and novel technical ideas as were exemplified in these prints. In this way tradition won out over the actual fact that here were some of the most thoroughly original and indubitably artistic prints of the century. I have sometimes wondered whether there is any field of art collecting which is more hidebound and hamstrung by arbitrary definitions than that of prints.

In any case, as seen from today's point of view, the great events in the nineteenth-century history of prints were the discoveries of photography and its attendant photo-mechanical processes. The tradition of snobbery is still so strong, however, that neither of these things is ever mentioned in any of the general histories of prints. Actually they have worked one of the major revolutions not only in vision but in the recording of its observations, and they have very completely changed taste and valuations in the field of the older prints.

As pointed out in the first chapter of this essay, the ancients had all the materials and basic techniques that were needed to make many kinds of prints. The one thing that they lacked was the idea of making prints. With photography, however, we come to a kind of print that no one could have made before the nineteenth century. The reason for this was that photography, instead of being based upon simple manual techniques and immemorially familiar materials, was based on quite recent developments in the sciences of physics and, especially, of chemistry. I have an idea that a very good argument could be put up for the claim that it is through photography that art and science have had their most striking effect upon the thought of the average man of today. From many points of view the histories of techniques, of art, of science, and of thought, can be quite properly and cogently divided into their pre- and post-photographic periods. It may be doubted if even the renaissance itself, or, if one prefers, the baroque seventeenth century, brought about such thoroughgoing changes in values, attitudes, and ideas, as took place in the nineteenth century and the early years of this one. Many of these new notions are intimately related to photography and its materials.

The prehistory of photography consists of two very different sets of observations, one of them optical, the other chemical. They were not brought into conjunction until the nineteenth century.

In all probability men have always wondered about the fact that when the sun strikes through an angular hole it makes a round spot of light on the surface it hits. Also many must have had the experience of seeing a brilliantly lighted street scene portrayed on the wall or ceiling of a darkened room by a beam of light that came through a chink in the window blind. It is said that

116

Daniel Barbaro's book on perspective, of 1568, was the first to point out that a sharper image could be procured if a proper lens were inserted in the chink in the window blind. This was the origin of the camera obscura, a name which is merely the Italian for a darkened room. In the eighteenth century and the early years of the nineteenth century the camera obscura was developed into a portable means of enabling people to take tracings of landscapes and other well-lighted subjects. Little practical use was made of it, and in general it was no more than a gadget for people who did not know how to draw. The only outstanding exception was Girtin, who, with its aid, produced one of the most remarkable sets of architectural etchings that has ever been made.

From the earliest times men have unavoidably been acquainted with the fact that some substances, such for example as human skin and freshly cut meat and wood, change colours when exposed for a while to the brilliant sun. In 1727, a German chemist named Schulze noticed that a liquid mixture of various things in a bottle became purple where it was exposed to the sun, but did not change colour where the sun did not strike it. He discovered that this was due to the presence in his mixture of a trace of nitrate of silver. During the rest of the century chemists recorded their discoveries of the action of the sun on a number of chemical salts. Among the other discoveries made by them was that of the existence at either end of the visible spectrum of invisible rays which affected their chemicals.

The first man, apparently, to try to put these experiments to practical use in picture-making was Thomas Wedgwood, who, in 1802, announced that he had been able to get an image of a leaf or other object that was laid on a piece of paper treated with nitrate of silver and exposed to the action of the sun. Where the sun hit the paper directly the paper turned dark, where the sun had to go through the leaf it turned the paper dark in proportion to the amount of light that went through it. Unfortunately, after a little while, the image of the leaf went dark also. Wedgwood and his collaborator Humphry Davy found no way of making these

117

images permanent, though Davy, later on, did discover that chloride of silver, when substituted for nitrate of silver, materially reduced the time required to get the image. Wedgwood also tried to make his images by exposing his sensitized paper to light in a camera obscura, but his chemicals were so slow in their reaction to the light that came through the lens of his camera that he did not succeed.

The story now divides into two quite separate and different parts, one of which led to the discovery of the daguerreotype and the other to that of the photograph. These are two very different things, and, in spite of long tradition to the contrary, should not be mixed up. A photograph is an image, usually on paper, in silver or pigment, or stain, that can be exactly repeated. The daguerreotype not only was not exactly repeatable, but its image instead of being composed of pigments or stains was made by the minute shadows cast by the light in microscopically small reticulations or pits in the surface of a highly polished metal plate. That this is so, is shown by the fact, discovered long afterwards, that an electrotype can be taken of a daguerreotype, and that the cast or mould made in this way also shows the image that is seen on the original daguerreotype.

As the making of daguerreotypes went out of fashion in the 1860's and has never returned, I shall deal with it first, so that later we may be able to get an uninterrupted story of the photograph.

Some time before 1826, Niépce, a Frenchman, discovered that a bitumen which was normally soluble in a certain kind of oil ceased to be soluble after it had been exposed to the sun. In 1826 he prepared a metal plate by covering its surface with his bitumen. He then waxed an old engraving, so that its paper became translucent. He put the waxed engraving on top of the prepared plate and exposed them together to the sun. Where the sunlight was prevented by the black lines of the engraving from reaching the bitumen, the bitumen remained unaltered, but where the light came through the paper the bitumen was made insoluble. Then by bathing his plate in his oil, he dissolved away the bitumen that lay under the lines

118

of the engraving. It was now a simple matter to bite the plate just as though it had been an etching plate, and to print from it in an etching press. One of the original plates is still in existence. The prints pulled from it were not photographs, but, curiously, were nevertheless the first crude instances of what today we call photomechanical process reproduction.

Niépce then carried the matter further. He coated a sheet of glass with his bitumen and exposed it for a long time in a camera obscura to the light reflected from objects. This time he seems to have got not only whites and blacks but middle tones between them in the coat of hardened bitumen left on his glass after he had bathed it in his oil. Niépce, however, kept his processes secret, and, as all the pictures of objects he made with them have vanished, the only record of his experiments is that which is contained in some very unrevealing letters and the lone metal plate and such prints from it as may exist.

In 1827 Niépce went into partnership with an inventive painter named Daguerre, but he died before the partnership produced any notable results. By 1837 Daguerre had produced a daguerreotype of a corner of his studio, by a process which he discovered by accident. He tried to keep his process secret even from those to whom he tried to sell it, and it was not until January, 1839, that, forced by a fire which had burned him out, he agreed to make his process public to the world in return for annuities to be paid by the French government to him and to the son of Niépce. The government had to look into the matter, and so it was not until August 19, 1839, that, at a great and theatrical meeting, attended by many notables and accompanied by all the publicity that was then possible, he demonstrated his process.

The daguerreotype plates had polished silver surfaces. These surfaces were exposed to the fumes of hot iodine, which covered them with minute dots of iodine which formed iodide of silver. The plates were immediately placed in a camera which had been already focussed on the object of which a picture was desired, and exposed to the light that came through the camera's lens. At that time it required, depending on the kind of a day it was, from five to forty minutes to make the necessary exposure. The plate was then immediately exposed to the vapour from a bath of hot mercury, which by forming an amalgam with the dots of iodide of silver that had been acted on by the light, made the image visible. To make the image permanent, it was necessary to get rid of the dots that had not been acted upon by the light. This was done by washing the plate in a bath of common salt, for which later on a bath of what we now call 'hypo' was substituted. The daguerreotype was thus a sheet of silver covered by an amalgam in which there were minute pits where the light had not affected the surface.

The detail and the accuracy of the pictures were astonishing, but the pictures were faint, they were in reverse, the tones were harsh, the surfaces were extremely fragile and could not be touched, and they could not be exactly repeated. Furthermore, the time required for the exposure was so long that it was impossible to make a portrait, let alone a picture of a human being or an animal in motion. Various people immediately attacked these problems with vigour. Bigger and more accurate lenses were made for the cameras which admitted more light and thus cut down the time required for an exposure. New ways of sensitizing the plates were discovered which made them much more rapid. By 1840 it was possible to take a portrait in a minute. The same year a way was found of toning the plates with gold, so that they were not so stark and harsh. In a very short time daguerreotypes were being made all over the world. Daguerreotype plates were worked up by etching and engraving so that they could be printed in the etcher's press. Prints of this kind appeared in a book printed at Paris in 1842. Among them were two, made by Fizeau, that might be called primitive photogravures. But in spite of everything, daguerreotypes were still in reverse, they were fragile, and they were not exactly repeatable. Their images could only be seen when the plates were held at such an angle to the light that it cast pale shadows in the microscopic pits in the surfaces. They were not photographs, and photography did not grow out of them.

While all this was going on in France, even more important things were happening in England. In 1833 William Henry Fox Talbot, a very remarkable country gentleman, was staying at Lake Como. He could not draw, but he wanted to make some pictures of the landscapes there, and so he tried to use a camera lucida. As in the case of many another man, the result of this was a great irritation. Talbot's mind turned to an old camera obscura that he had had many years before. While thinking about that he remembered 'the inimitable beauty' of the images he had seen in the camera obscura, and, to quote his own words, 'it was during these thoughts that the idea occurred to me . . . how charming it would be if it were possible to cause these natural images to imprint themselves durably, and remain fixed upon the paper! And why should it not be possible? I asked myself.' When he got home to England in 1834 he started to work. He repeated the experiments of Wedgwood and Davy, and went on from them. By 1835 he had discovered how to get images on paper of things he saw in the camera obscura. In that year he took a minute photograph of a leaded window in his house, and was pleased to note that when examined with a magnifying glass it was possible to count each of the several hundred panes in the window. More than that he had discovered how to make his images somewhat permanent, and, most importantly, he had found a way of exactly repeating them as positives. To do this he simply waxed his paper photograph, and, using it as a negative, printed positives from it on paper—as many as he wanted to make.

He used the process to make pictures of buildings and landscapes and pieces of sculpture and plants. These pictures he called 'photogenic drawings'. At last the problem that had defeated the Greek botanists, and that had been responsible for the difficulties of many of their successors, was solved. Talbot not only had an exactly repeatable image, but one that did not require the distorting services of either a draughtsman or an engraver. In 1841 he discovered that if, after making an exposure, he treated the exposed negative with a solution of gallic acid and silver nitrate, he could build up a very feeble, even an invisible, image into a strong one. He had discovered not only the latent image but the idea of developing or bringing it out. He called the results of his improved process 'calotypes', a word composed of two Greek words meaning 'beautiful images'. All these things taken together meant that Talbot had discovered the basic principles of photography as we know it today.

The permanence of the photographic silver image was assured by the use, suggested by Herschell, of what we call 'hypo' to dissolve out from the paper the silver salts that had not been affected by the light. Daguerre, when he learned of this, promptly adopted it for his process, but Talbot for a while kept on using his original solution of common salt, with the result that many of his early prints have faded away. Luckily, sharp photographs were taken of some of them before this happened.

Hearing of Daguerre's secret process, Talbot, to secure priority, read a preliminary paper before the Royal Society on the 31st of January, 1839, i.e. more than six months before Daguerre made his public disclosure. The following month, Talbot gave the same audience a description of his process, and demonstrated that he had secured some permanency for his images. The title of his first paper is interesting in itself—'Some Account of the Art of Photogenic Drawing, or the Process by which Natural Objects may be made to Delineate Themselves without the Aid of the Artist's Pencil'. In other words, he fully realized that these images which he made were not subject to the omissions, the distortions, and the subjective difficulties that are inherent in all pictures in which draughtsmanship plays a part. Here were exactly repeatable visual images made without any of the syntactical elements implicit in all hand made pictures. Had Talbot been an accomplished draughtsman instead of an incompetent one he would probably not have recognized this fact, even if he had discovered how to make the images.

Immediately after the announcements by Talbot and Daguerre many other investigators flocked into the fields that had thus been opened up. The two processes were rapidly refined and improved. But it was not until the 1860's that photography caught up with daguerreotyping in the favour of the public, which was primarily interested in portraiture and liked the minute detail of the daguerreotype, as well as its preciousness and fragility. The daguerreotype had stepped into the place previously held by the painted miniature. The calotype was used by D. O. Hill in 1843 to make what have become some of the most celebrated portraits that have been made in photography, but they did not then suit the public taste.

The story of the development of photography is clouded by the fact that many of the workers kept their discoveries secret, that others did not bother to give them adequate publicity, and that many of the discoveries were made almost simultaneously. Local patriotism has played its part in the stories as told by the historians. The long and short of it, however, was that ways were swiftly found of sensitizing various colloids, such as albumen, collodion, and gelatine, which could be applied to paper and to glass. New chemicals were discovered with novel photographic qualities. The emulsions became much faster, and sensitive to more and more of the spectrum. Originally the glass plates had to be sensitized and then immediately exposed while still moist. But ways were found of making plates that could be used dry, and therefore could be made and stored until they were wanted. They were soon being made and sold on the market. The same thing happened to the paper. The crux of the matter, in the competition between calotypes and daguerreotypes, was the fact that the calotypes being printed from rough paper negatives on a rough paper, were unable to produce the minuteness of detail that was the distinguishing mark of the daguerreotype. It was not until the glass plate and the shiny colloid surfaced paper had enabled the photographers to get detail comparable to that of the daguerreotype, that the battle was won for the photograph. We can see here the same factors at work that in the past had played such a determining role in the competition between the old graphic processes. Always the exactly repeatable image that gave the most detail in the same space won out.

Seemingly the first book to be illustrated with actual photographs was Fox Talbot's own *The Pencil of Nature*, which came out in 1844. Its illustrations were mounted calotypes. In 1847 William Stirling's *Annals of the Artists of Spain*—the book that discovered Greco, Velasquez, and Goya, to the English speaking world—made its appearance. The very rare fourth volume, of which only twenty-five copies were printed, contained a series of calotypes by Talbot after paintings and prints. Because of its method of illustration it is to be regarded as the cornerstone of all modern artistic connoisseurship, for it contained the first exactly repeatable pictorial statements about works of art which could be accepted as visual evidence about things other than mere iconography. It was no longer necessary to put faith in the accuracy of the observation and skill of the draughtsmen and the engravers. These reports were not only impersonal but they reached down into the personality of the artists who made the objects that were reproduced.

The early photographs were in black, or brown, and white. The negatives were, as the photographers say, 'blind' to the different colours of the spectrum except the blues and the violets—as is still the case with our ordinary modern photographic papers. Gradually, by the use of various stains, ways were discovered of making emulsions that were sensitive to the different colours of the spectrum in approximately their black and white values as seen by the eye. Thus it became possible to make photographs that showed white clouds against the brilliant blue sky, and in which the reds were not represented by blacks. It was not until it became possible to develop negatives in the dark by the present familiar 'time and temperature' methods, and without constant inspection by the trying light of the dark room, that it became possible to use these very sensitive emulsions to their full extent.

As early as 1810 Seebeck, in Germany, called attention to the fact that when a spectrum was thrown on a sheet of moist paper

124

sensitized with chloride of silver the paper took colours that were different in the different bands of the spectrum. Seebeck's investigations were followed by those of Herschell, in England, in 1839. In 1848, Becquerel, in France, succeeded in reproducing on a daguerreotype not only the colours of the spectrum but to some extent the colours of objects. It was not, however, until 1907 that Lumière, in France, introduced his method of making colour transparencies. It is only within the last few years that it has become possible to produce photographic prints in full colour.

As I have already pointed out, Bolton, in England, about 1860, succeeded in getting a photograph of a work of art on the surface of a wood-block, which he then engraved. Until the end of the century in England and America wood-engraving over or through a photograph printed on the face of the block remained the typical way of reproducing drawings, paintings, and photographs, for use as illustrations in books and periodicals. It was not until after the turn of the present century that the making and printing of half-tones was sufficiently perfected for them to yield brilliant impressions without supplemental re-engraving with the engraver's tool.

In 1839 Mungo Ponton, in England, discovered that when a coat of albumen on a sheet of paper was treated with bichromate of potassium any parts of the albumen that were hit by the light became hard and insoluble. Later, other experimenters found out that gelatine and other colloidal materials did the same thing. By mixing pigments with the bichromated gelatine it became possible to make photographic prints in any desired pigment. In the 1850's it was discovered that a coat of bichromated gelatine that had been exposed under a negative would hold printers ink on the parts that had been hardened by the light. Out of this came the first printing surfaces for the reproduction of photographs. They were what to-day we might call crude photolithographs. This technique was shortly followed by that which we call collotype. Next came that for the making of what today we call 'line blocks'.

William Blake, in the 1790's, had made relief etchings by

drawing his design on the copper with dissolved etching ground, and after it had hardened, biting out the spaces between his lines with acid. He used the method in his *Songs of Innocence* and later on in his various Prophetic Books. A photographic 'line block' of a line drawing is merely an adaptation of Blake's idea. The metal plates of the line blocks, from which the reproductions are printed, instead of having drawings made directly on them, are coated with some bichromated colloidal substance which hardens on exposure to light. The plate is exposed under a negative, after which it is treated in various ways, and then washed in water, which dissolves away the part of the coating that has not been hardened by the action of the light through the negative. It is said that Talbot was the first to do this. The plate is next treated with an acid-resisting substance which adheres to the remaining areas of the coating but not to the bare surface of the metal. It is then bitten in an acid bath which eats away the spaces between the lines. An edition of *Pablo de Segovie*, illustrated with line drawings by Daniel Vierge and published at Paris in 1881, has been said to be the first book illustrated with photomechanical relief etchings, but there is little doubt that the process had been well tried out before being used in such a book as that.

The greatest and most valuable of all the photomechanical processes, however, is that known as relief half-tone. Half-tones, with which we are all familiar in the common reproductions of photographs in our books, magazines, and newspapers, may be regarded as inverse aquatints made in such a way that they can be printed as relief blocks locked up in the printer's formes with type. It is in them that the aquatint with which Goya made his prints has come to its final great fruition.

In aquatint the irregularly shaped minute white dots are surrounded by wider or narrower lanes of ink—the white is always the solid white of the paper and the ink always a solid colour of the same tone or intensity. The appearance of changing tones is secured by the varying balance between the whites and the blacks, which themselves are always of the same unvarying tones.

It occurred to Talbot that it would be possible to make a photographic aquatint plate that could be used in the etching press. It also occurred to him that the dots in his aquatints would be more regular and dependable if they were made by the use of a screen instead of by the necessarily irregular methods of powdering the surface or flowing a solution of resin over it. In 1852 he took out a patent for using what he called a screen made either of textile or of ruled lines on glass. His scheme was to coat a plate with a bichromated layer of suitable colloid and then expose it to the light, first under a screen and then under a pictorial negative. Where the light came through the screen it would harden the coating in bigger or smaller dots according to the amount of light that came through the negative. Where either the screen or the negative kept the light from coming through, the coating would remain soluble. After the soluble coating was washed away it was an easy matter to bite the plate with acid in such a way that the lines between the dots were sunk below the surface of the plate. Talbot sent some prints made from such a printing surface to Paris in 1853.

Talbot's patent envisaged the making of intaglio printing surfaces, but the same technique was applicable to the making of relief printing surfaces. The early commercial half-tones, however, were made not with a screen but with rather a coarse aquatint grain. Easily available examples are to be found in some of the art journals of the early 1880's, such as *L'Artiste,* in which they were used to reproduce drawings by the masters. It would have been impossible to achieve comparable results by any of the older hand made methods of making relief blocks for book illustration. Poor as the blocks were, the only personal qualities visible in them were those of the men who made the drawings that were reproduced.

In the 1870's various experimenters began to use screens made of glass ruled with parallel lines, which sometimes were straight and sometimes were waved. This method, however, had its distinct drawbacks and limitations. In 1880 a New York newspaper ran the first cross-line half-tone to appear in a daily newspaper.

It was made through a screen of textile and was very rough and imperfect. In 1886 Ives, of Philadelphia, patented his idea of the modern ruled cross-line half-tone screen—which he produced by taking two sheets of glass, each of which was covered with ruled parallel lines, and fastening them together face to face in such a manner that their lines ran at right angles to each other. In 1892 Levy patented his method of ruling the lines on sheets of glass in such a way that the screens became both cheap and practicable. Before the outbreak of the first world war the ruled cross-line half-tone screen was in common use all over the world. The older generation of reproductive wood-engravers had nothing to do but die out, their hard-won art and craft a victim of what the engineers so simply call technological obsolescence.

The great importance of the half-tone lay in its syntactical difference from the older hand made processes of printing pictures in printer's ink. In the old processes, the report started by a syntactical analysis of the thing seen, which was followed by its symbolic statement in the language of drawn lines. This translation was then translated into the very different analysis and syntax of the process. The lines and dots in the old reports were not only insistent in claiming visual attention, but they, their character, and their symbolism of statement, had been determined more by the two superimposed analyses and syntaxes than by the particularities of the thing seen. In the improved half-tone process there was no preliminary syntactical analysis of the thing seen into lines and dots, and the ruled lines and dots of the process had fallen below the threshold of normal vision. Such lines and dots as were to be seen in the report had been provided by the thing seen and were not those of any syntactical analysis. If there remained the same complete transposition of colour and loss of scale that had marked the older processes, the preliminary syntactical analyses and their effects had been done away with, and the transposition of colours was uniform. At last men had discovered a way to make visual reports in printer's ink without syntax, and without the distorting analyses of form that syntax necessitated. Today we are so accus-

128

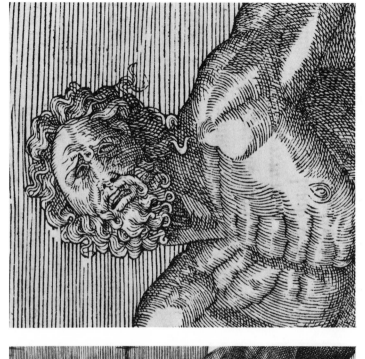

73A. The head of Laocoon, as engraved by Marco Dente, who died in 1527.

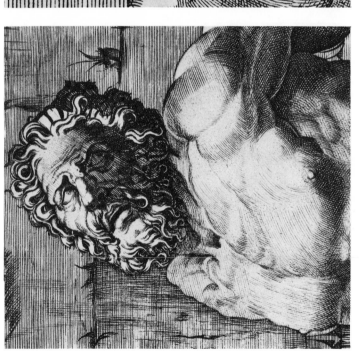

73B. The head of Laocoon as cut on wood for Marliani's *Urbis Romae Topographia*, Rome, 1544.

74B. The head of Laocoon, as it appeared in Sandrart's *Sculpturae veteris admiranda, sive delineatio vera*, Nuremberg, 1680.

74A. The head of Laocoon, as etched by Badalocchio, about 1606.

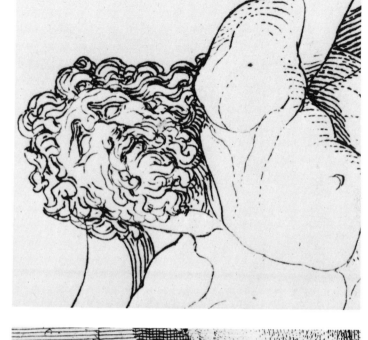

75B. The head of Laocoon, as it appeared in the *Musée Napoléon*, Paris, 1804.

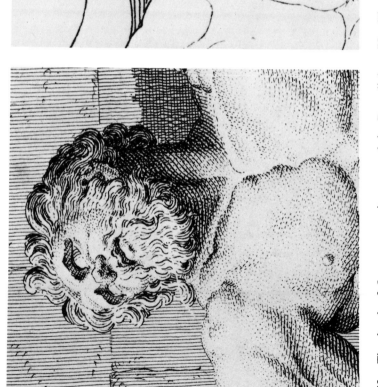

75A. The head of Laocoon, as it appeared in Poncelin's *Chef-d'oeurves de l'antiquité*, Paris, 1784.

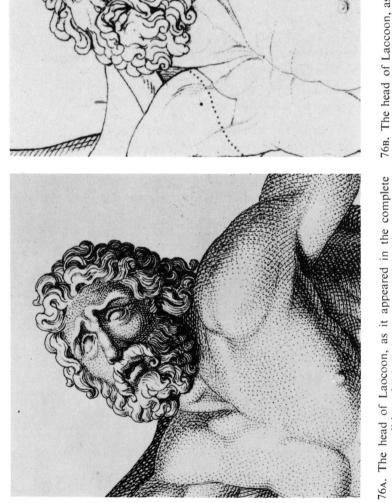

76A. The head of Laocoon, as it appeared in the complete edition of Winckelmann, Prato, 1834.

76B. The head of Laocoon, as it appeared in Clarac's *Musée de Sculpture*, Paris, 1839.

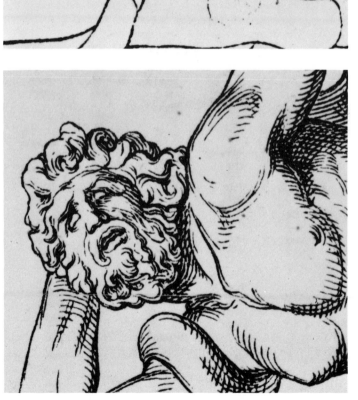

77A. The head of Laocoon, as it appeared in Lübke's *Grun-driss*, Stuttgart, 1868.

77B. The head of Laocoon, as it appeared in Murray's *History of Greek Sculpture*, London, 1890.

78. Detail from a mediaeval painted window, as reproduced in Mont-
faucon's *Monuments de la Monarchie Française*, Paris, 1730.

79. A classical head, as engraved for the Society of Dilettanti, London, 1809.

London Publish'd by Rich.d Lawrence,1.st April 1818.

80. Portion of an etching of the Parthenon Theseus, from R. Lawrence's
*Elgin Marbles*, London, 1818. Reduced.

tomed to this that we think little of it, but it represents one of the most amazing discoveries that man has ever made—a cheap and easy means of symbolic communication without syntax.

Great as was the change brought about by the pervasion of the Bewickian wood-engraving in the presses of the printers and the techniques of their use, that which was enforced by the half-tones was even greater. Paper-making underwent a very complete change, becoming ever more smooth and even in thickness. It is interesting to observe how few people realize the meaning of the fact that one of our modern line or half-tone blocks is treated as though it were a piece of type once it begins to be printed from. It is not only the largest piece of type the printer has to cope with, but from a strictly mechanical point of view the most difficult one that he uses. The half-tone may have anything from seventy-five to more than three hundred dots to a linear inch, each of which has its particular and essential size and shape that must be kept without change in the inking and printing, if the tints printed from the block are to be properly graduated and smooth. The printer has to adjust all his techniques of printing to the demands made by these particular printing surfaces. Had it not been for these demands many of the modern type printing processes would never have reached their present day mechanical perfection. It is all very well to talk about the pressmanship exhibited in the early printed books and in the books that come in limited editions from the modern special presses, but actually the pressmanship exhibited in any one of our modern large dictionaries or in many of our con-temporary newspapers, as for example, in *The Times*, of London, and in that of New York, is very much more remarkable.

We have seen how the older type presses were unable to cope with the problem presented by the larger wood-blocks that began to be made about 1820. The photomechanical blocks made a much greater demand for strength and precision than had been made by any of their predecessors. The design and the tooling of the old presses was loose and inexact and the thickness of the papers used was irregular and varying. To secure an even impression of the paper on the blocks and types it was necessary to interpose between the paper and the platen—i.e. the smooth surface of metal that squeezed the paper down on to the inked printing surfaces—a blanket or felt that took up all the little irregularities and maladjustments of the machine, the blocks, and the paper. Gradually the makers of printing presses and of paper discovered how to make them into instruments of a precision so great that the blankets (or soft pack) could be done away with. The problem was complicated by the need to run the presses at the high speeds required by the large sizes of modern editions. We are all aware of the difference between the accuracy with which the old horse-drawn vehicles were made and that which is essential to the motorcar, but very few of us are aware that a similar change took place in the mechanics of printing a generation before the motor vehicle came into common use.

With the gradual pervasion of the use of photomechanical processes of reproduction from relief blocks, first of line drawings, and then, through the half-tone, of photographs and wash drawings and paintings, it became obvious that most of the work that had been done in the past by the painters, draughtsmen, engravers and etchers, had basically been informative or reportorial rather than artistic in purpose, and that the new pictorial processes filled the pictorially informative needs far more accurately, far faster, and far more cheaply, than was possible with the other, older, techniques.

In spite of this evident fact, the tradition and the values of the past held on. The tradition said that engravings and etchings on copper and engravings on wood were not only the nice ways to reproduce pictures, but, more than that, the best ways. The fact that the old hand-made methods of reproduction never gave any indication of the surfaces and the tool marks in the originals was not regarded as of importance by the adherents of the tradition. I can well remember difficult conversations held less than thirty-five years ago with persons very highly placed in American art museums, who, still thinking in terms of the so recent, but already so dead, past, insisted that the best and the only really dignified way to reproduce important paintings and sculpture was to have them drawn by recognized artists and then etched or engraved by recognized etchers or engravers. One of these old fashioned gentlemen had actually, for a while before the first world war, been able seriously to hamper the library of his institution by his insistent and powerful belief that half-tones and shiny paper were nasty and should not be allowed to disgrace its shelves.

One of the ever recurrent arguments in the age long discussion and comparison of the different arts was the idea that, while words could give a sense of movement and development, the picture by its very essence was confined to a single moment. But photography was to change all that so violently that today it is to photography that we turn for all our studies and analyses of movement and action. There must be many hundreds of thousands of cameras in this country that, to use photographic jargon, can 'stop' a human figure in action at any point in its movement by taking so fast a picture of it that it appears to be perfectly still no matter how fast it is moving.

Oddly, the fastest way there is of taking photographs was, perhaps, the first fast one to be devised. As early as 1851, Talbot fastened a copy of a newspaper to a wheel that could be made to revolve with great speed. He focussed his camera on the newspaper, started the wheel to revolving, darkened the room, opened his camera, and took his exposure by the light of an electric spark. So far as we human beings are concerned the electric spark is pretty nearly the absolute in speed. When Talbot developed his negative he found that his exposure had been so much faster than the motion of the wheel that in the photograph the type of the newspaper could be seen—'every letter being perfectly distinct'. The latest developments of this method of what is now called stroboscopic photography have shown us the remarkable configurations which occur, for example, when a drop of milk falls into a saucer of milk or a golf club hits the ball. Photographs are essential to our studies of the air currents set up by projectiles and supersonic aircraft.

131

But fast single photographs only show the configuration at a single moment, so that it appears to be frozen. Recourse was therefore had to the old fashioned idea of the zoetrope, a toy in which a series of hand-made pictures were arranged on a drum which was then rapidly revolved. The pictures on the revolving drum melted into one another in human vision so that they gave the appearance of motion. The trick was, therefore, to get a series of photographs taken very fast and in very close succession. At first this was done by using a battery of cameras so arranged with a timing mechanism that their exposures were taken extremely close together in time. Muybridge was, perhaps, the first to use this method for a detailed study and analysis of the motions of men and animals. His investigations began in 1872, and his first set of photographs to be published came out in 1878. At least as early as 1879 he had devised what he called the zoöpraxiscope and combined it with an oxy-hydrogen light and a projection machine, in such a way that he was able to give extremely short 'movies' of men and animals in action. The idea, however, did not become practical until some years after Eastman, of Rochester, had in the 1890's devised methods of coating long strips of celluloid with a photographic emulsion for use in hand cameras.

By early in this century the moving picture in a very primitive form had begun to take a place in popular entertainment. At first one dropped a coin into a slot and peered through a peep-hole in a contraption to see a few seconds of moving picture. Nice people in those days regarded the thing as somehow beneath the consideration of serious persons—just as many of them did the motor-car. It took some time for the technique to be developed to such an extent that it became possible to give shows in theatres. Today it is not only 'big business' but the technique has taken its recognized place in many scientific laboratories, and it is used in educational institutions for teaching. The first movies were 'silent', then someone devised the 'sound track', which made it possible by photographic means to reproduce not only the figures and action of the persons represented but what they said or sang. This

81. Portion of a wood engraving of a drawing of the Parthenon Theseus, from Overbeck's *Geschichte der Griechischen Plastik*, 1869. Enlarged.

82. Portion of the etched state of an engraving, after Moreau le jeune, from the *Monument du Costume*, Paris, 1777. Enlarged.

completely changed the technique of the movie drama and made possible, for all sorts of purposes, such a recording of the faces, figures, action, and speech of men as had previously been undreamed of. Incidentally, the sound track can be changed without changing the photography of the action, so that the same movie with the same actors can be produced in as many languages as are desired, by 'dubbing in' different sound tracks. This has made possible a study of many things in linguistics that had previously been difficult of access. Among the amusing things it has brought out is that one of the most exacting problems the photographer in the studio has to cope with is the fact that the same things said in different languages take different times to say. Spanish is almost as fast as English. French is materially slower. And German takes a much longer time. Due allowances have to be made for this when 'shooting' the original action 'on the lot'. Today movies are made in full colour, as are also photographs and process reproductions of views and objects.

Daguerreotypes were taken through a microscope as early as 1839. Today microphotography is a regular proceeding in almost all laboratories, from those of the biologist to those of the metallurgist. It is said that Dr. Draper of New York was the first to take a daguerreotype of the moon. He did this in 1840, but it was too small to be of practical use. In 1865 a practically useful photograph of it was finally achieved. Today, at the great observatories, practically all the observations are made by photographic means. In actual fact, the enormous telescopes are merely camera lenses.

The light waves or rays at either end of the visible spectrum affect the photographic emulsions. Talbot was aware of this and, although he had no means of carrying his idea into practice, he imagined that photographs could be taken in complete visual darkness without the use of what we physiologically recognize as light. He called attention to this possibility as early as 1844. Today it is common practice to take photographs with the infra-red rays, which not only work in the dark, but penetrate through coatings of varnish that deface and cover old paintings and go through haze so that pictures of far-distant landscapes can be made. The infra-red rays are in regular use in hospitals, as are also the so-called X-rays. In 1895 Roentgen, in Germany, thanks to a lucky accident which he had the wit to follow up, discovered that it was possible to take shadowgraphs of things that were invisible to the eye because they were deep under the surfaces of things. The X-ray machine and technique have today become essential parts of the routine in hospitals, doctors' offices, art museums, and metallurgical shops.

Thus photography from being merely another way of procuring or making images of things already seen by our eyes, has become a means to ocular awareness of things that our eyes can never see directly. It has become the necessary tool for all visual comparison of things that are not side by side, and for all visual knowledge of the literally unseeable—unseeable whether because too small, too fast, or hidden under surfaces, and because of the absence of light. Not only has it vastly extended the gamut of our visual knowledge, but through its reproduction in the printing press, it has effected a very complete revolution in the ways we use our eyes and, especially, in the kinds of things our minds permit our eyes to tell us.

It has taken a hundred years of slow progress in the technology to produce this result, which, except for the flurry of excitement that accompanied the first announcements by Talbot and Daguerre, has come into being by such gradual steps that few people are very much aware of it. We take its results so much for granted that we never think of the situation before there was photography.

Thus we find ourselves in the peculiar dilemma of having a technical knowledge and capacity that are far in advance of many of our settled, accepted modes of thought and valuation, which have remained just as they were before even the initial steps were taken towards photography and are based on notions that in many respects are incompatible with its modern developments. I know that this is true in what is called art, and I have a suspicion that it is true in much of academic philosophy also.

# VII

## NEW REPORTS AND NEW VISION

## THE NINETEENTH CENTURY

A T the end of the nineteenth century photography had been known in one or another of its forms for sixty years, and some of the photomechanical processes for at least half that time. The traditional graphic processes had been defeated on most of what had been peculiarly and essentially their own ground—the making of exactly repeatable pictorial statements about the shapes and surfaces of things. The change had come about so slowly and gradually that, after the first explosion of interest and excitement which accompanied the announcements of Talbot and Daguerre in 1839, very few people were aware of what was taking place under, and especially *in*, their eyes. For a long time photographers were laughed at good-naturedly and were one of the stock subjects for jokes and caricatures. Slowly, as the community itself began to take photographs with hand cameras, there was no joke left because the photographer was everybody. As so many times before, men were doing something long before they knew what they were actually doing.

The photograph and its attendant processes took over at one

135

and the same time two very different utilitarian functions of the graphic processes that previously had never been clearly differentiated. One of these was the reporting of portraits, views, and of what may be called news. The other was the recording of documents, curios, and works of art of all kinds. Where the requirements of the first of these functions could be and still were on occasion fulfilled by the old techniques, the other had been taken over irretrievably by photography, for the photograph made it possible for the first time in history to get such a visual record of an object or a work of art that it could be used as a means to study many of the qualities of the particular object or work of art itself. Until photography came into common use there had been no way of making pictures of objects that could serve as a basis for connoisseurship of the modern type, that is for the study of objects as particulars and not as undifferentiated members of classes. The photograph in its way did as much for the study of art as the microscope had done for the study of biology.

Up to that time very few people had been aware of the difference between pictorial expression and pictorial communication of statements of fact. The profound difference between creating something and making a statement about the quality and character of something had not been perceived. The men who did these things had gone to the same art schools and learned the same techniques and disciplines. They were all classified as artists and the public accepted them all as such, even if it did distinguish between those it regarded as good and as poor artists. The difference between the two groups of artists was generally considered to be merely a matter of their comparative skill. They all drew and they all made pictures. But photography and its processes quietly stepped in and by taking over one of the two fields for its own made the distinction that the world had failed to see.

The blow fell first on the heads of the artists—painters, draughtsmen, and engravers—who had made factual detailed informational pictures. The photograph filled the functions of such pictures and filled them so much better and with so much

136

greater accuracy and fullness of detail that there was no comparison. For many purposes the drawing, as for instance in such a science as anatomy, preserved its utility because it could schematically abstract selected elements from a complex of forms and show them by themselves, which the photograph could not do because it unavoidably took in all of the complex. The drawing, therefore, maintained its place as a means of making abstractions while it lost its place as a means of representing concretions. The ground was cut from under the feet not only of the humble workaday factual illustrators of books and periodicals but of artists like Meissonier and Menzel, who had built up pre-photographic reputations by their amazing skill in the minute delineation of such things as buttons, gaiters, and military harness for man and beast. An etcher like Jacquemart had gained a world-wide reputation for his ability to render the textures and sheens of precious objects, such as porcelains, glass, and metal work—but when it was discovered that the photographic processes did all that infinitely more accurately than Jacquemart could, it was also realized that Jacquemart had been merely a reporter of works of art and not a maker of them, no matter how extraordinary his technical skill. The devastation caused by the photograph rapidly spread through all the gamut of the merely sentimental or informational picture, from the gaudy view of the Bay of Naples or the detailed study of peasants and cows to the most lowly advertisement for a garment or a kitchen gadget. What was more, by 1914, the periodicals had begun to be so full of the photographic pictures that the public was never able to get them out of its eyes.

The photograph was actually making the distinction that Michael Angelo had tried to point out to the Marchioness and her companions in the conversation that was related by Francesco da Hollanda—'The painting of Flanders, Madame . . . will generally satisfy any devout person more than the painting of Italy, which will never cause him to drop a single tear, but that of Flanders will cause him to shed many; this is not owing to the vigour and goodness of that painting, but to the goodness of such devout

137

person. . . . They paint in Flanders only to deceive the external eye, things that gladden you and of which you cannot speak ill, and saints and prophets. Their painting is of stuffs, bricks, and mortar, the grass of the fields, the shadows of trees, and bridges and rivers, which they call landscapes, and little figures here and there; and all this, although it may appear good to some eyes, is in truth done without symmetry or proportion, without care in selecting or rejecting, and finally without any substance or verve.' [1] Michael Angelo was attempting to point out that the pictorial report of things which people enjoy in stories and in actual life is not the same thing as design.

Inescapably built into every photograph were a great amount of detail and, especially, the geometrical perspective of central projection and section. The accuracy of both depended merely on the goodness of the lens. At first the public had talked a great deal about what it called photographic distortion—which only meant that the camera had not been taught, as human beings had been, to disregard perspective in most of its seeing. But the world, as it became acclimated, or, to use the psychologist's word, conditioned, to photographic images, gradually ceased to talk about photographic distortion, and today the phrase is rarely heard. So far has this gone that today people actually hunt for that distortion, and, except in pictures of themselves, enjoy it when found. A short fifty years ago most of the 'shots' of Michael Angelo's sculpture that were shown in the movie called *The Titan*, would have been decried for their distortion, but today they are praised. Thus by conditioning its audience, the photograph became the norm for the appearance of everything. It was not long before men began to think photographically, and thus to see for themselves things that previously it had taken the photograph to reveal to their astonished and protesting eyes. Just as nature had once imitated art, so now it began to imitate the picture made by the camera. Willy nilly many of the painters began to follow suit.

[1] Quoted from Charles Holroyd's *Michael Angelo Buonarroti*, London, 1903, by permission of Gerald Duckworth & Co., Ltd.

So long as the old graphic processes provided the only means of making exactly repeatable visual reports, men were always tempted to hypostasize something behind those reports that they could neither see, nor describe, nor report, but which was more real than the things actually contained in their reports. It was this unreachable, unknowable, *vraie vérité*, that all too often they tried to talk and argue about when they talked and thought about works of art with which they had not immediate first-hand acquaintance. When people begin to talk about nobility, grandeur, sublimity, ideality, and all that group of purely emotive verbal obfuscations, as qualities of art, the appreciation of art has become a sort of verbalist intoxication unrelated to particulars—a situation that is observable in the talk and writing of many persons who read books about art, or follow verbalist doctrines or party lines about it, instead of surrendering themselves to sharp-sighted first-hand acquaintance with it. It is interesting to notice how dry and tongue-tied so many of the people are who have had long and intimate first-hand acquaintance with works of art as compared with the volubility in abstractions of the persons who know about art through words and verbalist notions. Seen in its concretion, the greater a work of art is, the more it is a bundle, not of similarities to other things, but of differences from them. All that words can deal with, however, are similarities. The simple reason for all this is that words, with the exception of the proper names, relation words, and syntactical devices, are mere conventional symbols for similarities. Although differences are just as perceptible as similarities, the inability of words to cope with them has given rise to the notion held by many self-consciously hard-headed persons that talk about art is merely an attempt to deal with the ineffable, a thing that for them is completely laughable. But that these differences are not statable in words does not mean that they are ineffable, for they are clearly communicable in non-verbal ways. While the photograph is far from being a perfect report, it can and does in practice tell a great many more things than any of the old graphic processes was able to, and, most importantly, when two photographs of two different things that are very much alike are laid side by side, they enable us to gain awarenesses of differences that defy description either in words or in any of the old graphic processes that preceded photography.

In order to grasp the broad meaning of the photograph as record or report of work of art or curio it is necessary to look back over the nineteenth century, and to take account of some things that happened in it, apparently completely outside the territory that photography was taking over. I refer to the astonishing gathering together in the great capitals of Europe of the arts and crafts of the distant past and the far away, which was one of the distinguishing events of the century. It was greatly hastened, if not begun, by Napoleon, when, as part of his political propaganda, he systematically looted the countries his armies invaded, and brought back to Paris the results of his efforts. He did this not so much because of the artistic importance of his loot, as because it enabled him to demonstrate to both France and the world that he had been able to assemble in Paris the objects held most holy by the peoples of Europe. There was no comparable way of symbolizing the prowess of the Empire and the French. It was the nearest thing in modern times to the triumphs of the Roman generals and proconsuls, in which the kings, the high priests, and the most sacred objects of the conquered had been paraded before the Roman populace.

In the eighteenth century hardly anyone took seriously the art of the Middle Ages, let alone of the Dark Ages, except a few students who were interested in hagiography, iconology, and the lore of the local churches. A few dilettantes, such as Horace Walpole, were fashionably and perversely amused by the view from the Castle of Otranto, but for most of them, I think it can be said, the Gothic merely provided a relatively cheap way of being smart and different from other people. The rich who had received classical educations went in sentimentally for classical sculptures, which in practice meant Roman copies, either of the late Republic or Empire, or even of the eighteenth century itself, in which the Roman craftsmen so surprisingly and obligingly were able to

83. The same portion of the finished state of the same engraving after
Moreau le jeune. Enlarged.

84. A modern cross-line half-tone block after a photograph of a portion of Rembrandt's painting of 'An Old Woman Cutting her Nails'.

supply the northern nabobs with the very 'antiques' they were in search of. No one knew the difference between a Greek original and the ancient and modern imitation, as was demonstrated in such different ways by both Winckelmann, the founder of classical archaeology, who accepted fakes, old and new, and John Thomas Smith, who, in writing the life of Nollekens, told how that sculptor in his youth had paid his way by making modern ones. If we look at the pictorial reproductions of classical art that were available to collectors in the eighteenth century and much of the nineteenth century, we can discover not only many of the reasons for their blindness but the reasons they took their interest in the objects they actually collected.

The art of ancient Egypt was practically unknown until Napoleon made his armed descent into that country. He took with him a group of scientists, archaeologists, and artists, among whom was that very curious and interesting person, Vivant Denon— perhaps the first man to have a really catholic taste in art in our modern sense of the word. The difference between the seeing Denons and the posturing Walpoles of this world is rarely discussed, but it is very important. A great cargo of ancient Egyptian artistic and archaeological loot that Napoleon shipped for Paris had the misfortune to meet a British warship, with the result that, instead of going to Marseille or Toulon and thence to the Louvre, it went up the Thames and came to rest in the British Museum. Within a few years afterwards that institution also acquired, though in less exciting manner, the Elgin marbles and the friezes from Phigaleia, that were so remarkably unlike the classical sculpture which had been fashionable during the eighteenth century that some of the best judges of the day declared the Elgin marbles to be late work of the time of Trajan. If we are honest with ourselves, the Venus of Melos is a masterpiece not so much of ancient Greek sculpture as of the taste of the eighteen-thirties.

The French Revolution and the wars that accompanied and followed it caused many of the great church and monastic treasures to be thrown upon the market, with the result that for the first time in many generations there was available to the collector and the curious a flood of mediaeval works of art of all kinds, and of manuscripts and early printed books. The opening up to the curiosity hunter and the archaeologist of Greece, Egypt, and the Levant, was followed in turn by that of the Near East, and that in turn by that of the Far East and of southern Asia. Last of all to be recognized as works of art were the objects from America, Polynesia, and Africa, which had begun to accumulate in Europe as the result of exploration and armed adventure. The primary interest of those who brought most of these things back to London and Paris was not their artistic value but their curiosity.

In any case, nothing like this amassing of exotic objects had ever been known. One of the principal reasons it was so effective was that it was done by men who were so ignorant of art and taste that they gathered together everything of every kind without consideration of what the professors of art and the dilettantes might think of them. If the collections had been made in the field by the artistically educated of the day, very little that ultimately has been of great artistic interest would have been brought back. One can but imagine what such a pontiff as Ruskin would have acquired on the Guinea Coast or the islands of the Pacific.

So long as there were available only the traditional graphic processes of pictorial reproduction and publication the publication of all these strange things was not only very small in volume but very expensive and slow, and, worse than either, amazingly untruthful and distorted. As was inevitable, the print-makers rationalized their representations, and their rationality was that of their period. Also they liked to show what they imagined the objects looked like before they had been damaged or broken, and so they filled in the missing parts in their pictures out of the treasury of their ignorance, just as Thorwaldsen 'restored' the marbles from Aegina so thoroughly that he turned them into monuments not of Greek art but of early nineteenth-century taste. This desire to show ancient objects not as they have actually come down to us but as they ought to be, can be easily observed by attentive

142

visitors to almost any of our art museums. It flourishes most in those very collections or departments which take such great pride in their scholarship and the scientific quality of their knowledge that they look down on mere aestheticism. There is curiously little difference between much of the restoration done in museums and the faking done by the unregenerate.

The gradual introduction of photographic process in the last thirty years of the nineteenth century effected a most radical change in the methods of reproduction and publication of works of art. Not only did the reproductions become cheap, but they were dependable. Perhaps as easy a way as any to perceive this is to compare the illustrations of ancient and exotic art in the art books of the 1820's and 1830's with those in the art books of the 1870's and 1880's, and both with those in any cheapest little contemporary pamphlet or magazine. Until long after the middle of the century art books were much more a means by which the very rich could show their snobbishness than a means to convey truthful knowledge to the public. Actually the cheap modern photographic picture postcard contains so much more valid and accurate information than any of the expensive engravings and lithographs of the period of snobbery that there is no comparison between them. In this way photography introduced to the world a vast body of design and forms that previously had been unknown to it.

Objects can be seen as works of art only in so far as they have visible surfaces. The surfaces contain the brush marks, the chisel strokes, and the worked textures, the sum totals of which are actually the works of art. But the hand made prints after objects were never able to report about their surfaces. If the surface of a painting represented hair and skin, the print after the painting also represented hair and skin, but in its own forms and techniques which bore no resemblance to those embedded in the surface of the painting. In other words, the engraved representation of a painting was confined to generalized, abstract, reports about iconography and composition.

The magic of the work of art resides in the way its surface has been handled, just as the magic of a poem lies in the choice and arrangement of its words. The most exciting and the most boresome paintings can have the same objective subject matter. Their differences are subjective, and these subjective differences can only be seen in the choice and manipulation of the paint, that is in their actual surfaces. If Manet and Bouguereau had painted the same model in the same light, with the same accessories, and the same iconographical composition, any engravings made from them by the same engraver would have been remarkably alike. In a way the engravings were attempts, as the philosophers might say, to represent objects by stripping them of their actual qualities and substituting others for them—an undertaking which is logically impossible. The photograph, to the contrary, despite all its deficiencies, was able to give detailed reports about the surfaces, with all their bosses, hollows, ridges, trenches, and rugosities, so that they could be seen as traces of the creative dance of the artist's hand, and thus as testimony of both the ability and the deliberate creative will that went to their making.

The result of this is never referred to, but it was very important in the formation of opinion and values. Thus, to take a particular case: the engravings, saying nothing about surfaces, could easily be read, and actually were read, by a world soaked in the pseudo-classical Renaissance tradition of forms, as reporting that the sculpture of the early and middle Christian periods was merely a set of debased forms representing the inability of a degraded society and its incompetent artisans to hold to classical ideals and precedents.

With the advent of photography, however, it became impossible to maintain the opinions based on the engravings, for photography gave detailed reports about the surfaces of the Christian sculpture, with all their sharp incident, and revealed the skilful, wilful, way in which they had been worked. It thus became obvious that those works of art represented not any degeneracy of workmanship but the emergence and volitional expression of new and very different intellectual and emotional

144

values, and, therefore, had the right to be judged on their own merits and not from the point of view of the very ideals and assumptions which they challenged and against which they were engaged in an unrelenting warfare. From Winckelmann to the present day, the lack of expression and personality of the figures of classical art has been commented upon. It is the basis on which the archaeologists have built their claims for what they describe as the ideality of classical art. Christian art, however, in conformity with the faith it represents, developed the expression and personality of its figures and made deliberate sacrifices to that end. The photographic reports of surfaces made visible the volition with which this was accomplished.

Within the closed world of classical art itself the introduction of photography in place of the old engraved reports has had remarkable results. The inability of the engraving to report about surfaces and its restriction to iconography and composition made possible, in the early years of the last century, a sort of aesthetic transubstantiation. The discovery and bringing to western Europe of examples of Greek sculpture revealed that the actual qualities of fine Greek work were very different from those of the Roman copies with which Europe had been familiar up to that time, but the standard vocabularies, like the engravings which then provided the only available means of reproduction, were incapable of stating the differences. The result was that the world fitted the newly discovered qualities into the critical literary tradition and vocabulary of both words and pictures that had been built up about the so very different qualities of the Roman copies. No better example of the tyranny of the old methods of reproduction and their linear nets and syntaxes on the art of seeing can be desired than the dominance through the nineteenth century and into the present one of ideas and critical jargon that had their origin in the deficiencies alike of the Roman copies and the engravings after them. It is only within very recent years that the world has been able to see that the primitive Greek marbles and small bronzes were really very wonderful works of art. The current substitution of photographs of Greek pots for the familiar engraved and lithographic reproductions of dull routine modern drawings after them has brought about a notable change in the appreciation and understanding of their qualities.

Thus, luckily for the exotic and most of the early Christian and mediaeval objects, they were thought so lacking in beauty in the days of the engraved visual statement, that comparatively few of them were reproduced until after photography had taken over the task of reproducing works of art. Thanks to this they escaped the perversion both of form and of critical ideas that inevitably accompanied the older methods of reproduction.

A rarely mentioned result of this shift away from engraved reproductions is that the only prephotographic *catalogues raisonnés* of works of art that are still of use and constantly referred to are those of prints themselves. The photograph has antiquated all the rest. Its pervasion opened up the other subjects to visual scholarship as distinct from the scholarship of the texts and archives, and there began that flood of photographically illustrated catalogues and special studies that has enabled the vast masses of material to be reduced to order. It is astonishing to notice how few of the books, for example, about old Italian painting that were written before the eighteen-eighties are still referred to for qualitative judgments as distinct from purely archival matters. The rewriting of the inventory of old Italian paintings, that was made possible by photography, was so exciting that for several generations connoisseurs and students devoted their major efforts to problems of attribution, and even devised aesthetic theories which reduced subject matter and its imaginative treatment to a very subordinate and unimportant position. However, today, now that so much has been done on the new inventory, the special students of the younger generation are finding a new interest in iconography—the discovery of what it was that the old pictures illustrated.

Thus, while on the one hand the photograph enslaved a preponderant portion of the population to the photographic versions of natural forms, the photographic reproductions of curios and works of art emancipated an important group of people from the traditional and academic points of view. In many places, but especially in Paris, with its artistic confidence in itself and its faith that all had not yet been said and discovered in art, very intelligent men came to give serious thought to the aesthetic and other problems raised by these strange forms from the past and the far away. What took place in this group may perhaps be indicated to some extent by the mid-century story about Baudelaire and the naval officer. The officer had been away from Paris for a number of years on one of the exploring expeditions to the South Seas, and had brought back with him a great many strange objects. Baudelaire went to see him. Baudelaire was holding and looking very hard at a little carving when the officer, desiring him to look at something else which he regarded as of greater interest, referred to the object in Baudelaire's hand as 'merely a negro totem'. Instead of putting it down and looking at the other object, Baudelaire held up his hand and said, 'Take care, my friend, it is, perhaps, the true God.'

The formal academic art teaching and doctrine of the nineteenth century had been based on ideas that can be traced back to the Renaissance in Italy, and were full of assumptions that were believed in as indubitable truths. Some of these indubitable truths received very hard blows during the second half of the century, as for example, when the palettes were lightened, when pleineaireism made its first tentative appearance, when colours were broken down into their constituent shades, and when account began to be taken of such things as that shadows were very rarely or never brown. Many of these new ideas were based on notions derived from popular books on the physics of light and were defended as being highly scientific. Between the sharp-eyed notation of detail that was the mark of the English pre-Raphaelite painters and the new French interest in atmosphere and the envelope, as typified, for example, in the work of Claude Monet, there was little basic difference, great as was the superficial one. Each group believed in accurately reporting what it thought was the appearance of the thing seen. They merely happened to look for and to see quite different things and appearances. Where the pre-Raphaelites were greatly interested in the emotional implications of their subject matters, the French, realistically, contented themselves with ocular curiosity. But in each instance the emphasis was on verisimilitude and reporting.

One of the most important persons in the mediaeval royal courts was the king's jester, a functionary whose purpose was to keep the court amused, and who was privileged to utter home truths that would not have been permitted from the mouth of anyone else. I have little doubt that among the greatest influences in artistic Paris during much of the second half of the nineteenth century were the lithographed caricatures by Daumier. Daumier, in addition to being one of the caricaturists whose work reached the entire Parisian community two or three times a week, happened to be one of the boldest innovators of his generation and one of the great seminal forces in modern pictorial design. As caricaturist and funny man he was exempted from the trammels of pictorial convention which weighed so heavily on the solemn and the academic painters. He did with impunity things that had they been done in oil paint would have been shocking and inexcusable. The world laughed with him, the academic artists shuddered at the thought of him, and the intelligent saved and preserved his prints. When we think of the fate of most old newspapers, one of the wonders of the world is that such a vast supply of Daumier's caricatures was preserved. The print collectors did not care for the work of his maturity, because it did not conform to the wholly artificial notions they had conceived about what constituted good lithography, but many of the painters took his work seriously and studied it hard. Anyone who is familiar with the last fifteen years of Daumier's work can see the reflections of it all through the mature work of Degas, and consequently through the work of the younger artists whom he influenced.

Degas had an independent fortune and a witty and independent mind. His fortune did for him what Daumier's position as the accredited jester had done for him. He was enabled by it to go his own way without thought of the conventional modes of pictorial conduct on which the poorer painters depended for their sales. He was led by his study of the Italian primitives, of Daumier, and of the newly discovered Japanese prints, to think about the possibilities of what happened when compositions were built up about unfamiliar points of view, unconventional cutting of the field of vision, and the arbitrary use of colour. He and the group of younger artists who came under his influence were not only the greatest draughtsmen of their time but were also those who thought most about design. Their adoption of the unconventional point of view and unconventional cutting of the field of vision, and their willingness to invent colour schemes, enabled them to find visual interest and excitement in episodes from familiar life of a kind that had either been overlooked or had come to be regarded as exhausted. There is reason to think that Degas devoted so much of his attention to the ballet simply because its costumes, its attitudes, and the lights and the colours of the stage, bore so little resemblance to those of ordinary life that he could deal with them from the point of view of design absolved from the insistent popular demand for conventional verisimilitude. Gauguin had to go to the South Seas for similar release from the iron bound convention. Poor Van Gogh achieved it by going mad; Lautrec by becoming a social outcast.

In the Metropolitan Museum in New York there is a pair of pictures by Degas that remarkably illustrates his interest in this kind of thing. The basis of one of these pictures is a monotype in monochrome. The basis of the other is a counterproof of the same monotype. So far as their iconography is concerned they are mirror images of each other—exactly alike but in different directions. Actually they are so different that many people do not recognize their close relation to each other. Their colour schemes are absolutely unlike, and their masses of colour and light and shade bear no resemblance to each other. Had Degas not been over and above mere verisimilitude he could not have done them. Marvel-

149

lous as they are as separate works of art, taken together they demonstrate that Degas was primarily interested in design and not in representation. Had they become known to the world through engravings such as those that Raphael Morghen made after the great Bolognese painters the fundamental differences between them would never have been known to that part of the world which depended on engraved reproductions for its knowledge of paintings. Degas made a well-known remark that the ballet provided him with a '*prétexte pour le dessin*'. This phrase has been translated as a 'pretext for (representational) drawing', but the word '*dessin*' also means the very different thing we call 'design', which has strong creative, volitional, implications—and it was in this latter sense that Degas used the word. It was not his business to imitate what he saw but to dominate what he saw and to play with it as a creator of something quite his own.

In the 1890's and the early years of this century Toulouse-Lautrec made advertising posters with which the walls of Paris were covered. A Parisian might never have been to an art exhibition, and never have looked attentively at any painting, but he could not evade the Lautrec posters, for they were everywhere before his eyes. In them great liberties were taken with traditional forms and colours. Many of them were two-dimensional in design. And they had the great quality of 'carrying'—their arbitrary and wilful patterns could be seen from afar. The solemn and the traditionally minded did not take them seriously, but many picture-makers did. And they had their undoubted effects on the public's eyes. Just as Daumier, the jester, and Degas, the rich man, had been enabled to do many things that were not permitted to the painter who lived on the sale of his canvasses, so Lautrec, the witty advertising man, was permitted to do so too. The shock of his posters was for many people an ocular liberation. The public learned from them that verisimilitude was far from being the be-all and end-all of picture-making. Incidentally, these posters made it obvious to even the most obtuse that the Impressionist emphasis on the envelope was after all not much more than reporting and had not essentially altered the hardened tradition of picture-making—that actually Impressionism was only a technical variation on the standard academic themes, and that much of it was peculiarly empty.

Thus Degas and these younger men had discovered the difference between design and reporting, that a picture of gods and heroes and sentimental situations could be utterly trivial, and that a joke or a laundress, a bony ballet girl or café singer, or the good bourgeois and his wife, could provide the titular subject matter of as serious design as was ever contrived.

The ruling academic notions were based on silly theories about the dignity of subject matter and impossible ones about the truth of colours and shapes. Religious subject matter had begun to fall out of fashion before the end of the seventeenth century. It is doubtful whether any of the outstanding painters in France during the eighteenth and nineteenth centuries ever seriously put his mind on the traditional Bible stories from which the mediaeval and the Renaissance painters had drawn so much. Fine subject matter, other than portraits and landscape, had to be something far removed from the actualities of life, and preferably was to be taken from ancient myth or the lives of the heroes—the only subjects in which prudery permitted preoccupation with the nude female figure. As the ancient myths and the lives of the heroes were not generally known and certainly not emotionally cogitated over by the public, the dramatic element of picture-making gradually faded away. All that was left for the picture-maker-dramatist was a series of subjects that while apt to sloppy sentimentality were actually vapid and empty, because the pictures represented no one in particular. It is very difficult to arouse emotions about the human troubles and emotions of no one in particular. It may be that the frequent success of the mediaeval and later religious paintings was based on the fact that they represented very particular people about whom everybody knew and in whom everybody was very much interested—possibly the same reason that the ancient Greek drama in its time and way was so successful. In the failure to think about design all that was left was reporting of a kind that set great store by verisimilitude of a very limited and conventional sort. In the endeavour to accomplish verisimilitude it was overlooked that it can be acquired only at the cost of personality, with its emphases and omissions.

As to the truth of shapes and colours—the academic doctrine was based on a very complete contradiction in terms. What was thought of as visual truth was actually only a conventional verisimilitude, which was a very different thing. To leave colour out of the discussion for the time being, there is no such thing as a true still representation of a form in movement. Actually there is a constant conflict between the tactile-muscular sense returns and the visual returns, no matter how accustomed we may be to their association in what we think of as a single space. What we call the shape of a figure is no more than where its parts are in relation to one another at a moment. Its movement is how its parts are changing their relation to one another at a moment. The 'where' and the 'change' are incompatible notions, as has been known ever since the days of Zeno and his paradoxes. So far as the human eye is concerned it is impossible to see a shape clearly both in motion and at a moment. The camera has taught us that when we actually 'stop' the motion of an object completely enough to see its tactile-muscular shape with sharp accuracy, that is to say to stop it for something like the one five hundredth or the one one thousandth of a second which physiologically approaches a moment, the movement departs from both the perception and the record, and all we have is a stiff frozen shape that conveys no sense of motion at all.

The only way that a sense of motion can be given to a body in a still picture is by distortion of its tactile-muscular shape at a moment. We can see this in the very simplest of shapes, let alone in such complicated ones as those of the human body. It comes out in the difference between a fast and a slow photograph of the drops of water thrown by a lawn-sprayer. In the fast photograph the drops are clearly and sharply defined and betray no sense of movement at all. In the slow photograph the drops of water are blurred and elongated in the direction of their movement. It is this distortion in the picture that makes us feel that the spray is moving. The more we elongate our representations of rain drops the faster seems their movement. If we want to represent a terrific driving downpour we actually cover our picture with parallel lines running diagonally across it.

Much the same thing is true of colour. The only way we can get the colour of a spot is by matching it, which in practice means isolating it, but when we do that we change the apparent colour, for our perception of the apparent colour is affected not only by the colours of the adjacent areas but by their sizes and illumination. It is this, for example, that makes it impossible to get a true colour reproduction of even an abstract diagram in colour, let alone of a picture, unless we make our reproduction of the same size as that of the original and give it the same texture. There is literally no way to make a true colour reproduction on a changed scale. The implications of this should be obvious.

Another thing that the academics set up to do was to create beauty with a capital B. According to them beauty was something that the artist created. Beauty was the distinguishing mark of the work of the artist. But of course, it was only created by the real artist, who, also of course, belonged to the right trade union and abided by its rules and by-laws. From a logical point of view, I suppose, there has never been anything funnier than the idea of 'objects', the 'essence' of which was a 'quality' like 'beauty', for the making of which there were official recipes and cook books. Intrinsic beauty is today an exploded notion, though doubtless there are still many persons who believe in it.

Anyway, at the end of the nineteenth century and the beginning of this one, there were men in Paris who did not take the academics or their precepts and assumptions with any too great seriousness, and who did not hesitate to try to think about the problems presented by the arts of long ago and far away, with which they were gradually becoming familiar. Among other things these men perceived was the folly of the traditional view that the early and the exotic artists only worked the way they did because they were ignorant and unskilled, and that when we looked at their work we forgave them their errors because of their ignorance and their innocence—but that we should not forgive the work of contemporaries for such reasons. It came to be recognized in these inquiring circles which took design seriously that the primitive artists of Europe were not so ignorant and certainly not so innocent as the official academic painters believed. These groups also discovered that the Asiatics, the Polynesians, and the Africans were far from being all innocence in the ways they designed and carved objects. What these primitive and exotic artists had been ignorant of was the specifically western European post-mediaeval requirement of verisimilar reporting—an activity that had been taken over by the photograph.

Thus there gradually came into being a group of artists who were so much interested in this question of innocence and ignorance and knowingness in design and representation, that they began to make experiments for themselves to see whether they might find out why it was that objects that had no verisimilitude, that had lost all their anecdotal subject matter in their transference across the ages and the seas, and that ignored the canons of taste and beauty that had been set up in post mediaeval Europe, should nevertheless be so remarkably fascinating to the modern Europeans who looked at them. Of course these men talked and wrote as well as painted and sculpted, and of course much of what they said and wrote was arrant nonsense. For, after all, that is the way men have always gone about things of this kind. No greater nonsense has ever been perpetrated than that which great thinkers in the past have put forth in their search for workable hypotheses. But in the course of time something always comes out of these discussions and this kind of moonshine. What men do in these matters is what counts, and not what they say. And so, as we look back at what was being done about the turn of the century in Paris, we have to disregard the verbal notions and ideas and look at the things that were made. If we look at these dispassionately and without any doctrinaire *parti pris*, I believe we can see a pattern in them. This pattern is that of a long and exciting series of experiments and discoveries in syntax. It may be silly of me, but I cannot help being interested in the fact that these artistic experiments were being made just at the time that such men as Frege, and Whitehead and Russell, were making their syntactical analyses of the basic notions of logic and pure mathematics.

Just as the mathematicians and logicians in their investigations into the logic and syntax of arithmetic and geometry had to make a clean distinction between pure and applied mathematics and logic, in other words to omit all thought of the subject matters to which their mathematics and logic might be applied, so the artists had to give up thinking about anecdotal subject matter and verisimilitude in their experiments and investigations into the syntax of design. In this way they learned that many of the forms which had become traditional in the studios were not real in the sense of representing anything that was found in nature or of having any existence aside from their utility in the drawing school,—that actually they were merely syntactical devices, and that there were many variant varieties of them, none of them any truer than the other. In the abstract it is no truer that A times B equals B times A than that they do not equal each other. In practice it all depends on what you are trying to do, and you have the privilege of taking either assumption, as it meets your problem.

To object to these experiments on the ground that they did not conform to the accepted canons of reportorial representation was and is as foolish as it would be to object to the notations of the modern logicians because it is impossible to write a funny story or report an exciting fire in them. Just as there is a subject called the Foundations of Geometry, which bears little or no resemblance to the metrical geometry of the carpenters, so the work of these artists bore little or no resemblance to the factual reporting that most of the European world demanded of what it called art.

Naturally, as soon as these experiments were sufficiently

damned and belaboured a great many artists came into the game, not so much because they had any understanding of what it meant or represented, but out of curiosity, and in some instances because they mistakenly thought that it seemed to excuse incapacities in both draughtsmanship and design. It is to be doubted whether even the academics of the purest water misunderstood the movement any more thoroughly than did a lot of the most vocal of its fellow travellers. In any case, they seem to have been utterly unable to distinguish between the real and the imitation. There was, however, one peculiar difference between the men who started the investigations and the fellow travellers; the original group very rarely did anything that was deliberately offensive, or bilious, or resentful. Also, it was obvious, no matter how queer and odd their things may have seemed, that they knew very well how to handle their materials. Some of them were actually amazingly skilful draughtsmen even from the most reactionary point of view. Thus there was always a curious but indefinable sense of professional competence about their work. If it was shocking, it was not because it was in any way indecent or vulgar but because it challenged basic assumptions. It is funny how easily we forgive and forget nastiness and immorality, and how we harbour resentment against the men who raise questions that make us look foolish.

Today, as nearly as I can make out, the little drama has come pretty nearly to its end. People no longer get excited about it. But its results, I believe, have been a permanent gain, if in no other way than that the empty verisimilitude, the particular reportorial formlessness and lack of design which marked so much of nineteenth and early twentieth-century work of the defter and slicker kinds, has tended to find its level on the insurance calendars rather than on the walls of public buildings and museums.

I am convinced that all of this has taken place very largely because the photograph and photographic processes have brought us knowledge of art that could never have been achieved so long as western European society was dependent upon the old graphic processes and techniques for its reports about art. The syntaxes of engraving had held our society tight in the little local provinciality of their extraordinary limitations, and it was photography, the pictorial report devoid of any linear syntax of its own, that made us effectively aware of the wider horizons that differentiate the vision of today from that of sixty or seventy years ago.

# VIII

# RECAPITULATION

THE time has come to attempt a summary of the story and the argument that have so rapidly been indicated in the previous chapters.

While the number of printed pictures and designs that have been made as works of art is very large, the number made to convey visual information is many times greater. Thus the story of prints is not, as many people seem to think, that of a minor art form but that of a most powerful method of communication between men and of its effects upon western European thought and civilization.

We cannot understand this unless we bear in mind some of the basic factors in communication between human beings.

Whatever may be the psychological and physiological processes which we call knowing and thinking, we are only able to communicate the results of that knowing and thinking to other men by using one or another kind of symbolism. Of the various methods of making such symbolic communication there can be little doubt that the two most useful and important are provided by words and pictures. Both words and pictures have been known to man since the most remote times. In fact, it may be said that until the animal had used them he had not become man.

While both words and pictures are symbols, they are different

158

in many ways of the greatest importance. So little are they equivalent to each other that if communication were confined to either alone, it would become very limited in its scope. All words need definitions, in the sense that to talk about things we have to have names for them. Verbal definition is a regress from word to word, until finally it becomes necessary to point to something which we say is what the last word in the verbal chain of definition means. Frequently the most convenient way of pointing is to make a picture. The word then receives definition, or, if one likes, the thing receives a name, by the association of a sensuous awareness with an oral or visual symbol.

Any legible written word, whether it be drawn painfully by an illiterate or written in flowing calligraphy by a writing master, remains the same word no matter how it may look. The same thing is true of the sound of the spoken word, with all its personal peculiarities and local accents. The reason for this is that any particular specimen, whether spoken, written or printed, is merely a representative member of a class of arbitrary forms of sounds and visual signs, which we have learned or agreed to regard as having the same meanings. In every instance it is the class of arbitrary forms that has the definition as a word and not any particular oral or visual specimen. Thanks to this it is possible for a word to be exactly repeated, for what is given in repetition is not the same unique specimen but another equally representative member of the same class of arbitrary forms.

Hand-made pictures, to the contrary, we are aware of as unique things ; we all see the differences between them and know the impossibility of repeating any of them exactly by mere muscular action. Thus so long as the only way there was of describing objects was by the use of repeatable words and unrepeatable hand-made pictures, it was never possible from an oral or visual description to identify any object as being a particular object and not merely a member of some class. In thinking about this we have to remember that identification of the location, the function, or some particular marking of an object, is not a description of the object.

Except for the words which are proper names or syntactical devices, a word is merely a name for a class of relations, qualities, or actions. The consequence of this is that what we call verbal description is very often no more than the accumulation of a series of class names. It is much like the game we play on board ship when we toss loose rings of rope about a peg. No one of the rings closely fits the peg. If it did we could not toss it over the peg. As it is each ring can go over a great many very different pegs. But by tossing a great many very loose verbal rings over an object we think that we describe the object. Thus when we endeavour to make a full and accurate verbal description of even the simplest things, such for instance as an ordinary kitchen can-opener, we accumulate such an enormous and complicated heap of verbal rings that it becomes practically impossible for anyone but a highly trained specialist to understand what we have said. This is the reason the tool-maker wants not a verbal description of the thing he is asked to make but a careful picture of it. It is doubtful if any much more intricate intellectual process can be imagined than the translation of a linear series of verbal symbols, arranged in an analytical, syntactical time order, into an organization of concrete materials, and shapes, and colours, all existing simultaneously in a three-dimensional space. If this is true of such simple abstract forms as those of can-openers, it takes little thought to realize what the situation is in regard to the infinitely complex and accidental shapes that occur in nature and in art. It brings home to us the utter necessity of properly made pictures if we wish to convey our ideas in exact and meaningful ways. Certainly, without pictures most of our modern highly developed technologies could not exist. Without them we could have neither the tools we require nor the data about which we think.

Furthermore, science and technology, for their full fruition, need more than just a picture; they need a picture that, like the words of verbal description, can be exactly repeated. A word or a sentence that could not be exactly repeated would have no meaning. Exact repetition is of the essence for words, for without it they would be merely meaningless signs or sounds. Without exact repetition of the verbal symbols there would be no verbal communication, no law, no science, no literature. There would be only animal expression, like that of the barn yard. Over the years a good many people can see a picture, and many pictures can be sent travelling about the world. But, even so, a unique picture can make its communication to very few people, and it can only make it in one place at a time. There is a distinct limit to the number of persons who can seriously see and study and work from any single unique picture. As we have seen, the Greek botanists were fully aware of the limitation upon the use of hand-made pictures as a means of communicating exact ideas of shapes and colours. The reason for this limitation was that the Greeks, like their predecessors and, for many generations, their successors, had no way of making exactly repeatable pictures. They could only make copies of pictures, and when hand-made copies are made from hand-made copies it takes only a small number of copies for the final copy to bear no practically useful resemblance to the original. The meaning of this should be obvious so far as concerns the dissemination of accurate information about forms and shapes. In short, prior to the Renaissance, there was no way of publishing a picture as there was of a text.

While this is never mentioned by the historians of thought and art, of science and technology, it undoubtedly had much to do with the slowness of the development of science and technology and the thought based on them. Communication is absolutely necessary for scientific and especially technological development, and to be effective it must be accurate and exactly repeatable. Science in actual practice is not a dead body of acquired information but an actively growing accumulation of hypotheses put forth to be tried and tested by many people. This trying and testing cannot be done without exact repeatability of communication. What one or two men have thought and done does not become science until it has been adequately communicated to other men.

161

# RECAPITULATION

The conventional exact repeatability of the verbal class symbols gave words a position in the thought of the past that they no longer hold. The only important things the ancients could exactly repeat were verbal formulae. Exact repeatability and permanence are so closely alike that the exactly repeatable things easily become thought of as the permanent or real things, and all the rest are apt to be thought of as transient and thus as mere reflections of the seemingly permanent things. This may seem a matter of minor moment, but I have little doubt that it had much to do with the origin and development of the Platonic doctrine of Ideas and the various modifications of it that have tangled thought until the present day. The analytical syntax of sentences composed of words certainly had much to do with the origin of the notions of substance and attributable qualities, which has not only played a formative role in the history of philosophy but for long presented one of the most formidable hurdles in the path of developing scientific knowledge. At any rate, until comparatively recent times nominalism, with its emphasis on facts, its distrust of words, and its interest in how things act rather than in what they essentially are, has had little chance, and its great development has coincided remarkably with the ever-broadening development of modern pictorial methods of record and communication.

Some time at the end of the fourteenth or beginning of the fifteenth centuries men in western Europe began to make pictorial woodcuts, but no one knows when or where. For all we know it may have started simultaneously in many different places. By the middle of the fifteenth century men were engraving, and before its end they were etching. Printing from movable types began presumably in the 1440's; by the middle of the 1450's the Gutenberg Bible had been printed; and about 1461 the *Edelstein* came from the press. The *Edelstein* was merely a book of popular tales, but its pages were decorated with woodcuts. At the time they had no informational value or purpose. In 1467 the *Torquemada* was printed. It was a book of devotion, but illustrated with rough woodcuts representing definite particular things,—the pictures

162

with which a named and located church had been decorated. In 1472 the *Valturius* appeared. It was full of woodcuts of machinery, which were specifically intended to convey information. Shortly after 1480 the first illustrated botany book appeared. Its woodcuts were the last of a long series of copies of copies that started far back of the ninth century, and in consequence bore no relation to the things they were supposed to represent. In 1485 came the first printed botany book with illustrations drawn at first hand from the plants described in the text. In 1486 Rewich illustrated and printed the first illustrated travel book, the famous *Breydenbach*. Rewich had accompanied the author on his travels and drew the things they saw. In that same year three colours were first used in the printing of illustrations. In 1493 several illustrated catalogues of precious objects in the possession of some of the German cathedrals were printed. These appear to be the first printed illustrated catalogues of any kind of collections. By the middle of the fifteen-hundreds illustrated books about every conceivable kind of subject were coming from the presses of Europe in an ever increasing flood. Conspicuous among them were books about architecture, botany, machinery, anatomy, zoology, costumes, archaeology, numismatics, and, specially, some of the technologies and crafts. The single sheet print in the various mediums then available had begun its task of carrying across Europe in all directions information about buildings and works of art that themselves never travelled. The rapid pervasion of the Italian Renaissance and Baroque styles was accomplished by the single sheet print and the illustration.

Nothing like this had ever been known before. The same identical pictorial statements were made in each example of the edition, whether of a single sheet print or of an illustrated book. While for at least several thousand years men had been accustomed to having texts that repeated the same statements—Pliny the Younger, shortly after A.D. 100, referred casually to an edition of a thousand copies—now for the first time men were getting accustomed to pictures that repeated the same statements. It began to be possible to convey invariant visual information about things that words were incompetent to describe or define.

With few exceptions, these illustrations prior to the middle of the fifteen-hundreds were what used to be called 'facsimile woodcuts', i.e. woodcuts made by cutting away the surface of a wooden block between the lines drawn on it by a draughtsman. This was not a translation of the draughtsman's lines but a saving of them, as many of the woodcutters were so skilful that the 'hands' of the draughtsmen can be recognized in the prints from the blocks. This skill made it possible for first-hand pictorial statements to appear in books, not only in some volume or volumes but in every copy of the entire edition of a book.

The first-hand pictorial statement by a competent draughtsman has much the same value as the testimony of a first-hand witness. If he is sharp-sighted and observant he can tell us much about an object or an action, but nevertheless his training and habit of seeing and drawing lead him to select certain things for statements and to omit others from them. Each school of art had its scheme for laying lines, and these schemes in time became neither more nor less than grammars and syntaxes which, while making hand-made pictorial statements possible, also greatly restricted and influenced their power of statement. Much as he might want to, a German in the fifteenth or sixteenth century could not draw like an Italian, or *vice versa*. This meant that neither could say the same things in his drawings that the other could. We get sharp evidence of this in the copies that each made from the other—the Germans copying Italian engravings and the Italians copying German engravings. Although the specific lines of the original were there before him, the copyist never actually followed them closely in his copy, and rarely made any attempt to do so. Except in the most generalized of ways no two drawings, even one copied from the other, gave the same particularities. Especially was this true when the copy was not only a copy but a translation into another medium. The results of this are perhaps most easily to be seen in the prints after works of art, for in none of them are we able to find the kind of qualitative statement that is necessary for connoisseurship of the work of art itself. As represented in the prints it was impossible to tell the most arrant fake from the original.

However, no matter what its defects might be, the first hand visual statement in a print had the great advantage that it was exactly repeatable and invariant. This meant that in things like the descriptive sciences, such for instance as botany and anatomy, it was possible to produce what we may think of as representations that were standardized to the extent of the size of the edition. So long as the subject of the print was not a particularity but a generalized statement of the generic traits of some kind of object the situation was good enough. In fact, even today when we want to give a statement not of personal characteristics but of abstracted generic forms we still use drawings for our illustrations.

In the middle of the fifteen-hundreds several very important things happened in print making that were to have unsuspected results. The woodcut broke down under the constant demand for more and more information in the available spaces. To pack more pictorial information in a given space, the lines have to be made finer and closer together. This led to the making of wood-blocks with such minutely reticulated surfaces that for practical purposes the printers were unable to get good impressions from the blocks with the paper and the techniques of printing that were then available. Whereas it is easy to find copies of the earlier books containing good impressions of their coarser blocks, it is sometimes exceedingly difficult to find copies of later books that contain good impressions from their finely worked blocks. It is probable that many of the most important picture books of the mid fifteen-hundreds never contained good impressions from their blocks.

The engraving, however, did not suffer from this technical difficulty. Its lines could be very fine and very close together, as compared to those on any wood-block, and still yield a sufficient quantity of clear impressions on the papers then available. I think it can be said that this fact had much to do with the general increase in the use of engraving for illustrations that took place after the middle of the fifteen-hundreds. In any event, by the end of the century the engraving had taken the place of the woodcut in all but very few of the books made for the educated classes. This was not, as has been said, a mere superficial change in fashion, it was a basic change in modes and techniques made in response to an insistent demand for fuller visual information. In so far as there was a fashion as distinct from any need, I believe the fashion merely followed the norm set by the informational demand.

It thus becomes necessary to think about engraving and etching, which, from our present point of view, are to be regarded as varieties of the same technique. In the first years of engraving the engravers had been gold- and silversmiths. Then trained draughtsmen began to make engravings and, naturally, they used the linear schemes and syntaxes to which they were accustomed in their pen drawings and those of their schools. The German syntactical scheme was very different from the Italian. In the early years of the sixteenth century Marc Antonio and others after him began to make engravings after drawings, paintings, and sculpture by other men. These prints were made and sold not so much as works of art but rather as informational documents about works of art. Thus Dürer, in his Netherlands diary, refers to prints after Raphael as 'Raphaels Ding,' which he knew they were not. Marc Antonio evolved a novel scheme for the translation of sculpture into engraved reproductions. Instead of reporting about the surfaces of objects, their textures, their colour values, and the play of light across them, he devised a linear net which enabled him schematically to indicate their bosses and hollows. The most particular personal characteristics of the original works of art, their brush strokes and chisel marks, were thus omitted, and what was transmitted in the print was little more than an indication of iconography combined with generalized shapes and masses. At the end Marc Antonio used the same linear scheme in engraving Raphael's drawings and paintings that he had worked out for ancient sculpture—the characterless 'Roman copies' of Greek statues. It is important to remember this, for it had momentous consequences.

It is to be noticed that while the early engravers on occasion made prints of late mediaeval objects, such as Schongauer's 'Censer', it is difficult to find a reproductive print of such an object by any of the engravers who grew up in the linear syntaxes that came after Marc Antonio. For practical purposes it is impossible to find a reproductive print by one of the masters of engraving that represents an early painting or a piece of mediaeval sculpture. Such mediaeval statues as were reproduced were reproduced not carefully for their own sakes but merely as hastily indicated details in architectural ensembles. The vast number of these mediaeval things still in existence shows that they have always been held precious by somebody, if not as works of art at least as examples of skill, as antiquities, or as relics. Thus the lack of engraved reproductions of them cannot be explained simply on the ground of a change in taste or fashion. A much more likely explanation is to be found in the fact that they did not yield themselves to the kind of rendering which was implicitly required by the dominant and highly schematized linear practice of engraving. When you have no vocabulary with which to discuss a subject, you do not talk very much about that subject.

Marc Antonio's method was rapidly adopted and developed by engravers everywhere, for it had the great business advantages that it was easily learned and could be used, no matter how libellously, for many different kinds of subject matter. The very limited average instrument of a very limited average purpose, it became the dominant style of engraving in spite of the fact that it made it impossible for the engraver who used it to catch and hold the particular characteristics that gave the originals their unique qualities. Everything that went through the procrustean engraving shops came out of them in a form that had been schematized and made reasonable—and reasonability meant conformity to the generalized abstract conventional webbing of lines that was an

167

incident of manufacture. As every great work of art is as by definition unconventional in its most important aspects, a representation of it in terms of a convention that leaves out those aspects is by definition a misrepresentation.

Shortly after Marc Antonio began his grammatical or syntactical investigations, the print publisher and dealer began to make his appearance. He was a manufacturer-merchant, and often was not himself an engraver. He employed others to make prints, not of subjects that interested them, but of subjects that he thought he might be able to sell. Very often that could have been the only interest that he himself took in them. Some of the publishers had the engravers work for them in their shops, just as though they had been mechanics. As ideas of business efficiency came in, the engraver gradually ceased to make the drawings after the originals he 'reproduced'. The publishers procured drawings of the objects they wanted to make reproductions of. These were then handed to the engravers, who copied and translated them on to their copper plates, generally without ever having seen the objects their work was supposed to represent. The consequence was that the prints which came out of these efficient shops were at best second or third hand accounts of their distant originals, and, not only that, translations of translations as well as copies of copies. The scheme of operation made it impossible to give any pictorial report of such things as the brush work, the chisel strokes, or the surfaces, of the originals—which, in fact, were the originals. Moreover, the prints became filled with clichés of representation based on the requirements of the linear syntax that had been adopted by the engraving craft, which interposed a flat veto on the representation of the most personal of all the traits of the original work of art. The linear network varied but little in its general scale, although the objects that were engraved, be they large or small, were all reduced or enlarged to a few typical scales which had no relation to the sizes of the originals. This had important effects on the vision of the people who used the engravings.

Naturally this schematic network of lines became the medium for the exhibition of a great deal of virtuosity, not of keen reporting but of the handling of the lines in the network. The extravagances of the virtuosi had their immediate effect on the day's work of the more humble artisans of the copper plate. The textures of the network became ends in themselves and not merely aids to statement. Form and content were separated, and both got lost.

When engraving became a capitalist enterprise it became important to get as many impressions from the engraved or etched copper plate as possible with as little difference as might be between them. Towards the end of the sixteenth and the beginning of the seventeenth century this problem was worked at with great business acumen by a number of men in different places. Among these men there may be mentioned Rubens, the painter, Callot, the etcher, and Abraham Bosse, who wrote the standard technical treatise on the craft. These men invented and rationalized ways of laying and sinking lines on plates in such a way that the plates would yield very large editions before they wore out. This not only affected the weave of the linear net, but increased its independence from accuracy in reporting.

Rubens, if not actually the first important artist to have a financial interest in the reproduction of his work, was the first to create about himself a school of engravers who specialized in the reproduction of his pictures, and often was himself either the publisher or a partner in the publishing firms. Anthony van Dyck, his famous painter pupil, used the services of a group of these engravers of the Rubens school to produce a set of over a hundred portraits, the first few of which he himself had etched. The set ran through many editions, and its coppers were still being printed from in the present century. The influence of the set can be traced in many engraved portraits until the second half of the nineteenth century. In a way it may be regarded as having provided the norm for much of subsequent portrait-engraving and etching.

In France, the only country that had a single artistic capital, engraving had a popularity perhaps greater than it enjoyed anywhere else. The French engravers of the seventeenth century embarked on a search for linear methods that would be economically efficient and at the same time afford opportunity to show off their skill and agility in the choreography of their self-assumed goose-steps. Their skill in these goose-steps soon became of more importance than the fidelity with which they reproduced their originals. Some of them engraved in parallel lines, others evolved elaborate schemes of highly artificial cross-hatchings, some became experts in the sheen of satins and metal and the barbering of hair. The subjects to be engraved were undoubtedly chosen to enable them to shine in their specialties. Few of the masterpieces of art did this.

In the eighteenth century the French fashion for framed drawings in interior decoration led to the attempt to give closer reproduction of the superficial qualities of the drawings that the engravers worked from. Up to this time engravings had looked like engravings and nothing else, but now, thanks to the discovery of new techniques, the test of their success began to be the extent to which they looked like something else. Among the new techniques used for this purpose were aquatint and stipple, and soft ground etching, the crayon manner, and others still. Some of the plates began to be printed in colour the more closely to imitate the drawings and water-colours. In the seventeenth century mezzo-tinting, a blurry medium devoid of sharp accents, had been invented as a way of reproducing oil paintings in tones instead of in lines. Except in England, where painting was lower in key than in France, it was not much used. One of the curious things about all these new techniques of making prints is that so little original work was ever done in them. Goya was the only great artist ever to produce more than a sporadic essay in aquatint. The best artists to make more than an odd soft ground etching were Girtin and Cotman. Turner made a few reproductive mezzotints after his own drawings. But I doubt if any great artist has ever regularly used any of the other methods for his first-hand expression. I think it can be said that as a rule the great artist has habitually used only such graphic pro-

170

cesses as are comparatively direct, and that the desire for expression is incompatible with the indirections, the technical complexities, and the linear routine that mark most of the reproductive techniques. Direct a process as engraving was in the hands of the primitive masters, and notably in those of such men as Pollaiuolo and Mantegna, it is to be noted that from the point of view of the artist the 'facsimile woodcut' was still easier, for all that he had to do was to make a stylized drawing on the block which was then cut by a skilled mechanic. Even such a complete master of the technique of engraving as Dürer actually designed many more woodcuts than he made engravings, and, if we omit six or eight of his most popular engravings from the count, his most interesting work was done on the block. A further reflection of this easiness of the woodcut is to be seen in the fact that Holbein and Burgkmair made no engravings, and that Baldung and Cranach made but a very few. The wide spread of etching among original artists in the seventeenth century and again in the nineteenth century can probably be accounted for by the fact that it was the most direct and simplest method of making printing surfaces that was known prior to the invention of lithography.

However there is no getting away from the other fact that the easiest way for the original artist was to have his work copied by the professional reproductive engravers. The result was that by the end of the eighteenth century single sheet prints and book illustrations had, with few exceptions, become mere second- and third-hand statements, in which everything had been reduced to the average common-sense level of craftsman's shop work. By the end of the eighteenth century the first-hand visual statement had practically ceased to exist in the illustration of books, and in the single-sheet print it had become the rare exception. In France, at least, the manufacturing situation in the engraving shops had become even more complicated than it had been in the past, for the printing surfaces were often made by several men, beginning with an etcher, who laid in the outlines of the print from the drawing, and winding up with a finisher-engraver, who went over the etched lines and filled in between and reduced everything to the neat, tidy, characterless, and fashionable, net of rationality of engraving. Sometimes some equivalent of the quality of the drawings for the engraver made a ghostly flicker in the first etched states, but by the time that the finishers had done their work of degradation all qualitative equivalence to the originals and to the drawings for the engraver had completely vanished. The things that counted in public estimation were the brilliant moiré of the damask of the engraved lines and the sentimentality of the general situations represented.

I personally have no doubt that the growth of pictorial reasonability in the eighteenth century was based on the economics and shop practices of the business of print manufacture. Neither have I any doubt that this business had a great effect on the public as well as on the artists, for it was through the engraved picture that the world received its visual notions about most of the things it had not seen and studied with its own eyes—which is to say about most of the things in the world. One might think, if one had not waded through the contents of some of the great historic collections of old prints and illustrated books, that any visual report of a work of art would always tell much the same story about it, no matter where or when it was made, but the fact is that the reproductive prints and illustrations contained far more of the linear syntaxes and shop practices of their places and times of production than they did of the detail or character of the originals they purported to represent. Actually the buyers had come to appreciate prints and illustrations far more for the skill of their makers in the artificial dance steps of the engraver's tool than for any representational fidelity.

Then the poor and the uneducated did not have reproductions. But the rich and the educated did, and their reproductions had a great effect upon their vision, which, as today, was based not so much on acquaintance with originals as on acquaintance with reproductions. I have spoken of the net of engraved lines and all that it omitted, but there was another equally important factor for vision in the old engraved reproductions. The sizes of the printed reproductions bore no necessary relation to the sizes of the originals. In the printed picture the great mural might easily be smaller than a little portrait, a jewel greater in size than a façade. Further, in the hand-made reproduction all trace of the handling of his tools by the maker of the original had vanished. There was no difference in the engravings between the texture of a painting by a young Raphael and that by an aged Titian, or between the surfaces of a 'Roman copy', a Greek original, and a Gothic sculpture. The wilful theatrical stroke of Rubens's brush in one of his sketches, like the dominant expressive gouge of Michael Angelo's chisel, was smoothed out and obliterated. If the original artist had resorted to shorthand in his statement of any form, the engravers spelled it out at length in terms of the most commonplace vision and cliché of rendering. Had the engravers worked from the originals more than they did, and less from poor sketches by poor draughtsmen, this might not have happened to the same extent. But, whoever might have tried it would still have faced the problem of the longevity of his plates, and that absolutely required the artificial net work of line. Steel facing was not discovered until photography was in use.

As it was, a blighting common sense descended on the vision of the educated world. This showed itself not only in the terms in which that world talked about art but in the contemporary art the world relished. Its principal interest had been diverted by the means of reproduction away from the actual qualities of the originals and works of art and directed to generalized notions about their subject matters. Thus the century failed to take account in art, just as so much of it did in writing, of the thing that Pascal, in the seventeenth century, had pointed out about writing—that the quality of a statement consists more in the choice and arrangement of the particular symbols used in making it than in its general sense (*Les sens recoivent des paroles leur dignité, au lieu de la leur donner*). The eighteenth century talked about harmony, proportion, dignity, nobility, grandeur, sublimity, and many other common-sense abstract verbal notions based upon the

173

gross generalities of the subject matter that came through into the engraved reproductions. The sharp particularities of which works of art are necessarily constructed and which give them their character and value were unknown and unmentioned, for they escaped verbal description and were never reproduced in the reproductions. Thus, in spite of Winckelmann's remarks about engravings and the necessity of knowing the originals, the aesthetic doctrine of his *History of Ancient Art* of 1764 may be regarded as the rationalization of a set of values based on the catch of the engraver's net. The same thing can be said of most of the critical discussion in such a standard book as Bosanquet's *History of Aesthetic* which was published in 1892, i.e. at a time when the photomechanical processes were still in a very unsatisfactory state of development. It is amusing to think how few of the great weavers of aesthetic theory had any familiar first-hand acquaintance with works of art and how many of them either, like Lessing, knew the art they talked about only through engravings, or else sieved their ideas out of the empty air. Had it not been for this it is doubtful whether the Milords who made the grand tours would have been so happy and complaisant about all the poor copies of High Renaissance pictures and all the bad 'Roman' imitations of classical sculpture which they brought back to the North.

We can catch a glimpse of what was going on in still another way. Very few of us ever think to what an extent the painters of the fancy subjects and historical compositions, which were so generally admired during much of the eighteenth century and the first part of the nineteenth century, produced their canvasses to be engraved rather than to be seen in their paint. The sale of the painting was often of less importance than the sale of the prints after it. Hogarth knew this very well. The patronage of Mr. Alderman Boydell, the great print publisher, meant more to many an English painter than did that of His Majesty and a dozen dukes. Today in America we have a curious analogue in the novelists who write for the sale of their 'movie rights' rather than for the sale of their books.

# RECAPITULATION

At the end of the eighteenth century a number of things happened which were to have remarkable consequences. Men discovered that, by using the engraver's tool on the end of the grain of the wood instead of a knife on its side, it was possible to produce wood-blocks from which the finest of lines and tints could be printed in great quantities. Paper, smooth paper, began to be made by machinery run by power in a continuous process. Iron printing presses came into being, and in 1815 one was invented that was run by power and not by the strength of men's backs. The number of impressions that could be run off in an hour was greatly multiplied. Stereotyping was remembered and put to practical use. In 1797 Senefelder discovered how to make lithographs; Wedgwood in 1802 announced the first practical step towards Talbot's later discovery of photography. By early in the 1830's the book publishers had discovered that there was a great market for cheap illustrated books, magazines, and cyclopaedias, directed at the man in the street and not at the classically educated gentleman in his elegant library. Among these publications were many that dealt with techniques and the processes of making and doing things, and it was not long before the ordinary man, the uneducated man who used his hands and who knew how to read and to look intelligently at explanatory pictures, was finding out much from which he had been effectually debarred. The crafts instead of being the 'arts and mysteries' of highly restricted trades and guilds were thrown open to anyone who had the ability to teach himself from a book. Out of all this came such a rush of inventions and new processes as had never before been known. The same thing happened in many of the sciences and for much the same reasons. At least in England, which took the lead in all this invention and investigation, the outstanding engineers and scientists for a long time were not the graduates of the classicizing 'public schools' and the universities, but the ingeniously self educated. It had great moral and ethical results, as well as economic and social ones.

In art, the lithograph made it possible for such artists as Goya

175

and Delacroix to send out into the world their own drawings, not in unique specimens but in editions. Each impression had all their personality and all their daring, unhampered and unspoiled by the intermediary engravers. Things like Goya's 'Bull Fights of Bordeaux' and Delacroix's illustrations for *Faust* blew a great hurricane through the dead air of the single-sheet print and the book illustration in France. It shortly produced Daumier.

In the 1830's Talbot and Daguerre worked out photography and the daguerreotype, and in a little while it became possible for the first time to have reproductions of works of art that had not been distorted and vulgarized by the middle-man draughtsman and engraver—to have reports of works of art that had not been reduced to the syntax and the blurring technical necessities of a manufacturing trade and craft. For the first time it became possible to have a reproduction of a drawing or a painting or a piece of sculpture that told enough about the surface of its original for anyone who studied it to tell something about the qualities of the original. By the third quarter of the century many experiments had been made towards getting the photograph translated into printer's ink without the intervention of either the draughtsman or the engraver. About 1860, Bolton, an English wood-engraver, thought of having a photograph made on his block of wood so that he could engrave a piece of sculpture without having to get a draughtsman to draw it on the block for him. This eliminated one of the two chief obstacles to getting truthful reproductions into the pages of books. Bolton's method remained the principal way of making book illustrations until the end of the century. In the seventies attempts were made to produce what we now call half-tones. This came to fruition in the eighties and nineties with the invention of the ruled cross-line half-tone screen, a device which made it possible to make a printing surface for a pictorial report in which neither the draughtsman nor the engraver had had a hand. Its great importance lay in the fact that the lines of the process as distinct from the lines of the visual report could be below the threshold of normal human vision. In the old hand-made processes the lines of the process and the lines of the report were the same lines, and the process counted for more than the report in the character of the lines and the statements they made. Until after the two sets of lines and dots, those of the process and those of the report, had been differentiated and separated and the lines and dots of the process had been lost to ordinary vision, as they are in the photograph and the fine half-tone, there had been no chance of getting an accurate report. Man had at last achieved a way of making visual reports that had no interfering symbolic linear syntax of their own. In the whole history of human communication it is doubtful if any more extraordinary step had ever been taken than this.

Within a very few years the new method had overrun the world. Not only did it revolutionize printing, but it gave such accuracy of reporting as had never previously been dreamed of. It was prerequisite to the existence of all our popular magazines and of our illustrated newspapers. It has brought about a very complete restudy and rewriting of the accepted history of the arts of the past, and more than that it has made all the exotic arts known of the ordinary man. It is interesting to notice how few of the books of connoisseurship published prior to 1880 are still either authoritative or on the shelves for ready reference. The very vocabulary of art criticism has been changed, as have the qualities for which men look in works of art. Whatever else 'aesthetics' may now be, it is no longer a scholastic quasi-philosophizing whose task is to justify a tradition of forms based in equal measure on obstinate ignorance and sacro-sanct revelation.

The flood of photographic images has brought about a realization of the difference between visual reporting and visual expression. So long as the two things were not differentiated in the mind of the world, the world's greater practical and necessary interest in reporting had borne down artistic expression under the burden of a demand that it be verisimilar, and that a picture should be valued not so much for what it might be in itself as for the titular subject matter which might be reported in it.

177

# RECAPITULATION

The photograph and photographic process having taken over the business of visual reporting from the hands of the pictorial reporters and the engravers, the artists suddenly found themselves absolved from any need of verisimilitude in their expression and design. A great many of them, knowing nothing whatever about either expression or design, were lost, for they too had been members of the public and had regarded verisimilitude as the purpose and the justification of their work. Except in the work of the very greatest artists, creation and verisimilitude are incompatible, contradictory aims, and it is only at the hands of these greatest artists that creation has won out in the conflict between the two. With the photograph the magic dance of the creator's hand became for the first time visible in the reports of his work. Thus photographic reproduction of works of art and of what used to be called 'curios' has raised basic questions about the validity of many of the most hard-shelled and firmly entrenched doctrines about both art and beauty. It has changed Asiatic and African, Polynesian and Amerindian curiosities into works of art. It has revealed to the public for the first time something of the actual qualities of the Greek and later European arts of the past. It has brought about not only a reconsideration of the curious and ambiguous notion of the masterpiece—which often was no more than the object or picture which particularly lent itself to the linear net of the engraving—but it has caused many famous and adulated things to fall from grace and bestowed grace upon many unknown ones. It has made the western European world see that 'beauty', as it had known it, so far from being something universal and eternal was only an accidental and transient phase of the art of a limited Mediterranean area. Beauty is no longer the absolute that the pontiffs for so long proclaimed it to be. The photograph has made it obvious that what for four centuries the European world had acclaimed as purpose and beauty in art was no more than a peculiarly local prejudice about subject matter and mode of presentation. I think it is clear that this prejudice was to a great extent based on the methods of reproduction through which artistic and factual report alike had reached the public. For generations that public had been circumscribed and made provincial by the limitations imposed by the syntaxes of its graphic techniques. It is significant, for example, that many line engravings of nudes are 'good', and that very few in any of the other techniques are. The nude was the particular fish for which the net of engraving had originally been devised. In the photograph the nude is more than apt to become either a 'naked' or a vulgarity. The nude has ceased to be the great preoccupation of the artists that it was before the pervasion of photography.

For centuries the European world had been unable to distinguish between factual reporting, with its necessary requirement of verisimilitude (of which perspective was an essential part), and that expression of values, of personality, and of attitude towards life, with which verisimilitude is always at war. As the elder Haldane once remarked, 'it is only through the constant negation of mere appearance that personality realizes itself'.[1] At last, thanks to the photograph, visual dream and expression were no longer required to conform to the informational reportorial demands of the ordinary businesses of life.

In addition to all this, the exactly repeatable pictorial statement in its photographic forms has played an operational role of the greatest importance in the development of modern science and technology of every kind. It has become an essential to most of our industries and to all of our engineering. The modern knowledge of light, like that of the atom, would have been impossible without the photograph. The complete revolution that has taken place in the basic assumptions of physics during the last fifty years could never have been accomplished without the data provided by the photographic emulsion.

The total effect of all these things upon technical philosophy has been remarkable. Many of the old problems, the 'perennial problems of thought', now seem in a way to be resolved by the

[1] Quoted from J. S. Haldane's *Life, Mechanism and Personality*, by permission of Mr. John Murray.

179

discovery that at least some of them are little more than accidents of unrecognized, unanalysed syntaxes of symbolization.

The seriousness of the role of the exactly repeatable pictorial statement in all the long development since about 1450 has escaped attention very largely because that statement has been so familiar that it has never been subjected to adequate analysis. Having been taken for granted it has been overlooked. The photograph, as of today, is the final form of that exactly repeatable pictorial statement or report. Although it has very great limitations, it has no linear syntax of its own and thus has enabled men to discover that many things of the greatest interest and importance have been distorted, obscured, and even hidden, by verbal and pictorial, i.e. symbolic, syntaxes that were too habitual to be recognized. It is unfortunate that most of the world is still unaware of this fact.

In a way, my whole argument about the role of the exactly repeatable pictorial statement and its syntaxes resolves itself into what, once stated, is the truism that at any given moment the accepted report of an event is of greater importance than the event, for what we think about and act upon is the symbolic report and not the concrete event itself.

# INDEX

181

# INDEX

# INDEX

188